God So Lo

After doctoral research in org...   ... Atkinson
trained for the Church of Eng....u priesthood and served in
parishes in Bolton and Birmingham. He moved to Oxford in
1977, to become Chaplain at Corpus Christi College, where he
was subsequently a Fellow and Lecturer in Theology. He has
been Visiting Professor at Hope College, Holland, Michigan.

In 1993, David was appointed Canon Chancellor of
Southwark Cathedral and Missioner in the Diocese of Southwark, and from 1996 has been Archdeacon of Lewisham. He
has published a number of books and papers in Christian Ethics
and Pastoral Theology as well as some expository biblical
studies. David is married to Sue, who is a freelance education
writer and lecturer, and they have two grown-up children.

For Roy and Anne

GOD SO LOVED THE WORLD
TOWARDS A MISSIONARY THEOLOGY

David Atkinson

LYNX

First published in Great Britain 1999
Lynx Communications
Society for Promoting Christian Knowledge
Holy Trinity Church
Marylebone Road
London NW1 4DU

Bible quotations are from the *Revised Standard Version of the Bible*
© 1971 and 1952, unless otherwise stated.

The author and publishers would like to thank the following
for permission to reproduce material in this book:
'Do Not Go Gentle into That Good Night',
Dylan Thomas, *Collected Poems*. Published by JM Dent
and reproduced by permission of David Higham Associates.

British Library Cataloguing-in-Publication Data

A catalogue record for this book is available from the British Library

ISBN 1-901443-16-7

Typeset by David Gregson Associates, Beccles, Suffolk
Printed in Great Britain by Biddles Ltd, Guildford and King's Lynn

CONTENTS

Contents

Contents

PREFACE

I used to be a researcher in organic chemistry, and was asked recently to write an article for a magazine describing my journey from science laboratories to being an archdeacon in the Church of England. One of the people who read it said, 'That may be all very well for you, but some of us have real difficulty in believing impossible things.' I realize that the White Queen was able to believe at least six impossible things before breakfast, and that I simply may not have had enough practice. But I, too, find it hard to believe impossible things. To believe in the God and Father of our Lord Jesus Christ, however, is not impossible to me, but (despite all the difficulties, questions and uncertainties) it is by far the most reasonable way of making sense of the world I find myself in. I want to try to say why, and this is one of the purposes of this book. I want in particular to explore 'glimpses of God' in the ordinarinesses of life, in religious experience, in science, morality and personal relationships.

Another purpose of this book is to attempt to explore the connections between a reasonable faith and the tasks of Christian mission. This will take us into discussions about the changes in contemporary culture, the questions of ethics, and the practice of spirituality, for it seems to me that all these belong together as different facets of one diamond. What we believe, how we behave, how we pray, what we do are as inextricably linked as are the dimensions of the command to love the Lord our God with all our heart and soul and mind and strength. So I want to probe the meaning and nature of the Church's mission in a constantly changing world.

The outcome of these explorations is, I hope, a pointer towards what David Bosch once called 'a missionary theology'. By that he meant not just a theology of mission but a missionary agenda for theology. As he intimated, theology really has no business to exist other than critically to accompany the church in its mission to the world.

I would like to express my thanks to The Revd Jerry Lepine, Southwark Diocesan Adviser in Evangelism, and to Dr Anne Richards of the Church of England Board of Mission, both of whom kindly made helpful comments on an earlier draft of this manuscript, and especially to Bishop Roy Williamson, formerly Bishop of Southwark, whose invitation to work as Canon Missioner forced me to think about these things in fresh ways, and whose friendship, encouragement and support I greatly value.

David Atkinson
August 1998
The Feast of St Aidan, Bishop of Lindisfarne, Missionary, d. 651

INTRODUCTION
MISSION AND THE MODERN WORLD

It is a commonplace to remark that we are living at a time of unprecedented change, the pace of which is sometimes breath-taking. Some of the changes are social, some technological, some in the realm of ideas and the ways we think and decide about things. Some are immensely positive, creative and life-enhancing. Others are more ambiguous. And some are destructive of human well-being and social cohesion.

There are, for example, social changes, which include family patterns, sexual habits, and the growth in the proportion of elderly people and in the social and financial costs of care. There are changes in the worlds of education, health care, work, leisure and unemployment. There is a growing gap between rich and poor and there is the rise of the 'lottery' culture. There are changes in the institutions that foster personal relationships and community health, together with a loss of trust in 'authority'.

There are technological changes, which in medicine, for example, include embryology and cloning, which raise questions about parenthood and about personal identity. The human genome project gives us power to manipulate the human future for good or ill. The growth of information technology makes global communication increasingly easy, but it also makes buying and selling information into the new currency. The growth of media monopolies means that no one knows who is telling the truth. The power of media soundbites too easily reduces communication and argument to trivial rhetoric and point scoring. As with most advanced industrial societies, the British economy is rapidly changing us from producers into consumers. There is pressure to think of everything primarily in financial terms, and our worth as people too quickly becomes measured in economic and functional units.

There are changes in the area of language, with the growth of the priority of the visual over the verbal, of image over substance. The distinctions between fact, fantasy and 'virtual reality' become blurred – how do we tell the difference? The rapid decline in institutional religion is coupled with the rapid rise in fringe religion: paganism, Satanism, New Age, astrology, the occult, new religious movements. The National Lottery has even been described as a new religious movement, with its new foundation for life, hope, changed values, changed lifestyle and so on, as well as massive built-in disappointment, addiction and social divisiveness.

All this, and of course so very much more, is taking place in the context of enormous political and economic global changes in which questions of nationhood, monopolies, industrial institutions, the stewardship of earth's resources and the future of the planet are all in flux.

In and through all this change, there are stories of individual people and of human communities, living their lives, coping with their uncertainties, creating their futures. Some are flourishing, joyous, embracing change for their good and the good of others. Some are crushed, struggling, suffering, uncertain. There is ambiguity in the world, and paradox. The twentieth century has seen the most remarkable of human inventions, the most devastating of human tragedies, the most evil of human cruelties. What meaning do we give to this world of unprecedented change?

What is less often remarked within Christian circles is that such changes inevitably put large questions to the faith and message of the Christian Church, and as to how the Church goes about its ministry and mission. How is 'the faith once for all delivered to the saints' (Jude 3) to be believed and shared with coherence and meaning in the contemporary world?

Before we can begin to address that question, we need to unpack further some of the more radical changes in our cultural ideology and world views which underlie much of the change we have been discussing. In particular, we need to look at the shifts taking place from what is often called 'modernity' to 'post-modernity' – and to the major questions which these changes pose for Christian faith.

Modernity and post-modernity

By modernity I mean that pattern of social life, thought and values which has dominated Western Europe for the past two hundred or more years – the world in which modern science and technology were born, the world of the industrial revolution, of democracy, of the rise of the significance of the 'individual'. Modernity, which flowed from the Enlightenment, called in question many Christian assumptions.

Now, I do not want to be misunderstood at this point. There is a very great deal in the development of Western culture since the Enlightenment for which we thank God. There are many reasons for gratitude in the recovery of the significance of each individual person, the development of science and technology (with the impact that has made on industry, medicine, transport, education and many of the facilities of contemporary living), the birth and development of democracy, the flowering of many aspects of art, literature and music. All this is gain, and there is very much more. However, these gains were bought at the expense of some significant changes in Western culture, changes which from the perspective of Christian theology were not all unambiguously positive. It is these less comfortable (from a Christian point of view) features of 'modernity' which have sometimes tended to cast their spell over the whole of our culture.

For our purposes in this book, we will pick out five main aspects of modernity, namely:

- ideology
- moral understanding
- patterns of social life

- rationality
- idea of progress

As we will explore in more detail in a moment, the following are the sorts of issues I mean. In *ideological* terms, modernity can be thought of in terms of a shift from understanding the world in terms of the 'big Story' of God's purposes, to one based on other interpretative stories centred in human reason or human will. In *moral* terms, the shift was from a Christian view of morality as something given and objective, to a 'modern', subjective view of morality as something we decide for ourselves. In *social* terms, there was a significant shift of emphasis from a theological understanding of human persons as essentially relational, made in the image of God the Holy Trinity, to an emphasis on the importance of the individual. In terms of *rationality*, there was a movement from the idea of human reason as a response to the truth about God's world to the idea of human reason as something to do with our controlling the world through our thinking and then our science and technology. What we may call 'instrumental reason' took centre stage. Finally, the Christian concept of *purpose*, related to the doctrine of God's *providence*, was replaced by an optimistic belief in human progress, thought of as the inevitable result of human autonomy, individual freedom and technical mastery. There was much more to the project of the Enlightenment than this, of course, and such a cursory summary has the potential for being more misleading than helpful. But the inescapable fact remains that very significant changes in these five aspects of European culture were taking place from the Enlightenment onwards for the next two hundred years, and these changes called seriously into question many of the theological assumptions of a Christian view of the world. We will pick up these themes again shortly.

In the last two decades even more significant changes have been happening. Many recent thinkers have suggested that modernity has become exhausted, its enchantments broken, its hopes unfulfilled, and that we are now into a phase of rapid transitions into what is often called post-modernity.[1] This is that development within, or sometimes rejection of, the culture of modernity which offers a wide range of different intellectual, moral, political and social options, many of them despairing, some more hopeful, in their place. We can suggest three main sorts of reaction to modernity.

First, some of the reactions to modernity have replaced its inappropriate human-centred optimism with a view of the world which is ultimately nihilistic and despairing. They have massively rejected the Enlightenment heritage, and, in terms of culture and the ways in which we think and speak and write about life and death and depict them in art and literature, have turned their back on the Enlightenment. The philosopher Nietzsche seems to have come into his own in some of these writers of post-modernity.

Second, there are those who are more optimistic, and are reacting to modernity by seeking to hold on to its positive and critical contributions to our culture, while recognizing that some of its enchantments no longer hold us under its spell. They are trying to recover the good aspects of the heritage of the Enlightenment, to hold on to the benefits of modernity, and to answer post-modern critics by reaffirming modernity's values.

Third, there are yet others who are looking for a recovery of an appropriate 'big story' which again gives us grounds for acknowledging an objective morality, the importance of community, the reframing of rationality and the recovery of purpose. Those in this group are dissatisfied with the heritage of modernity, and are not at all persuaded by the despair of much of post-modernity. Some of this third group are responding to the challenges of post-modernity by effectively trying to become 'pre-modern' again. At its worst this can be a naive, ostrich-like way of responding, by pretending that the twentieth century never happened. But there is a more responsible, critical and careful way of responding to the questions posed by modernity and post-modernity, and that is by seeking to recover some of the benefits and values of the pre-modern world, but doing so in a way that is fully aware of and alive to the critical questions posed by the Enlightenment, and to the fact that we are now living in a very different world.

All this has resulted in a melting-pot of ideas which can be frightening and overwhelming, but is also hopeful. All the boundaries seem to have gone, the markers moved, the certainties no more. Many of our earlier ways of thinking and speaking and writing about life and death are called in question. Yet it is precisely this ferment of ideas which opens the way for a renewed opportunity for the Christian story to be told freshly once more, and which, I believe, is grounds for significant hope.

It is my conviction that the Christian gospel is at the heart of a reasonable faith – one that enables us to make most sense of the world we are in – and that the Christian Church needs to recover its nerve about the gospel, and about the confidence with which its faith is shared. It is faith in a God who in one sense is changeless, and in another is a God of change. It is a faith with crucifixion at its heart, which does not slip glibly over the pain, the tragedy, the sheer incomprehensibility of suffering. It is a faith which engages with the confusions, paradoxes and contradictions of the struggle of living in this world. It speaks of a God who enters into this world's suffering, abandonment and death, but a God who also transforms, heals, makes things new. It is faith in a God whose grace, so believers have testified, holds them in life and in death. I believe it is a faith to be shared, and that the Church needs to engage more radically with the implications of that faith for its life and mission in the post-modern world. But I believe the Church also needs to engage more radically with the questions which the post-modern world poses for its life and mission. Some of the chapters which follow try to back up my conviction that faith in God is reasonable, and also in the light of that, and interwoven with that, try to explore the implications of that faith for the contemporary mission of the Church.

One of the basic themes which underlies this book was wonderfully expressed in the second century by Irenaeus, Bishop of Lyons, when he wrote: 'The glory of God is a living man' (Irenaeus, p. 490). He was speaking of the humanness of Jesus Christ, in whom the glory of God is most

clearly seen. A more colloquial, but perhaps even more powerful translation reads: 'The glory of God is a human being fully
alive.' As I shall try to illustrate, one of the goals of the mission
of the Church is to enable human beings individually and
within their communities to display the glory of God by
becoming more fully alive.

For the rest of this introductory chapter I want to stand back
to look first at the Christian meaning of mission and then at
some of the questions put to contemporary Christian faith by
the changes in ideology, morality, social patterns, rationality
and ideas of progress in the contemporary world. That will
then set our agenda for the rest of this book.

So, some words about mission.

What is mission?

'Mission' is first and foremost a word about God. As we know
the word 'mission' comes from the Latin for 'to send' (*mittere*),
and mission has what has appropriately been called a centrifugal aspect to it. Mission is about sending out, not about
dragging in. I stress this because I was at a clergy meeting some
while ago, talking about the job I was doing then as Canon
Missioner and saying certain things about mission. At the
end of my talk, one of the quite senior priests present said,
'You'd never get people here to come.' I said, 'To what?' 'To a
mission – marquee on the common, crooning choirs – won't go
down very well here.' I thought he was having me on, but no,
despite my efforts for the previous 20 minutes, this was what
the word 'mission' meant to him.

So let me be quite clear what the word 'mission' means to
me. It is about God, and the outflowing of God's love.
According to the New Testament, the Father sends the Son
into the world; and sends the Spirit onto the disciples. The
disciples are then sent out by the Father, in the name of the Son
and in the power of the Spirit, for the sake of the world. A key
text for me is Jesus' words recorded at the end of John's Gospel:
'As the Father has sent me, so I send you' (John 20.21). In the

Gospels, Christian discipleship is often introduced with the words of Jesus: 'Follow me.'

Mission is the mission of God in Christ, empowered by the Spirit. The Church's mission is to discern what God is doing in the world, and be caught up into that mission of God in Jesus Christ, whom the Father sent and who now sends us. In its inadequate, partial and struggling following of Jesus, it is to be a mirror of the life of God.

If we were to ask the authors of the New Testament, 'Why was Jesus "sent"?', they would, I think, answer in at least three ways: to save, to serve, to liberate.

First of all, the word 'sent' is related to God's action in sending his son to *save*:

> God so loved the world that he gave his only Son, that whoever believes in him should not perish but have eternal life. For God sent the Son into the world, not to condemn the world, but that the world might be saved through him. (John 3.16–17)

If the Church, empowered by the Holy Spirit, is to be caught up into the mission of God in Christ, we will need to be caught up into the saving ministry of Jesus. This means that we will need to be concerned not only with relationships with God, but with relationships between people and within communities. Our agenda will cover themes such as reconciling, saving from sin, alienation, making things right between people, forgiveness.

Second, Jesus Christ describes his mission as being sent to *serve*: 'The Son of man also came not to be served but to serve.' 'I am among you as one who serves' (Mark 10.45; Luke 22.27). If the Church is to be caught up into the mission of God in Christ, we will need also to talk about sharing in the serving ministry of Jesus. We will have to ask what it means to be on the side of the poor and disadvantaged; how to fulfil the command – with towel in hand – to wash one another's feet. This will take us into – among other things – issues of community care and service to our neighbours.

Third, the Gospels depict Jesus as the *liberator*. Jesus himself says:

> The Spirit of the Lord is upon me, because he has anointed me to preach good news to the poor. He has sent me to proclaim release to the captives and recovering of sight to the blind, to set at liberty those who are oppressed, to proclaim the acceptable year of the Lord. (Luke 4.18–19)

Once again, if the Church is to be caught up into the mission of God in Christ, there is a liberation dimension to her mission. We will be concerned with the pastoral ministry which offers release, healing and liberty to people. But we will also set the saving and the serving in a context of concern about the injustices perpetuated in the wider society. We will need to engage with the ecological questions raised by living on this planet and how, as stewards of God's creation, to safeguard its future. We will have an eye to the economic and political dimensions to living in God's world.

Following the 1988 Lambeth Conference of Anglican bishops, the report *The Truth Shall Make You Free* reaffirmed the following widely accepted marks of mission.[2]

The mission of the Church is:

1 to proclaim the good news of the Kingdom;
2 to teach, baptize and nurture new believers;
3 to respond to human need by loving service;
4 to seek to transform unjust structures of society.

To this was later added:

5 To strive to safeguard the integrity of creation and sustain and renew the life of the earth.

The authors go on to say that we see signs of the Kingdom's presence, as Jesus promised:

- when men and women, being justified by faith, become a new creation in Christ;
- when women and men are being healed at their deepest spiritual, physical and emotional levels;
- when the poor are no longer hungry and are treated justly as God's beloved;
- when the Church takes seriously the formation of women and men into the likeness of Christ through the work of the Holy Spirit;
- when unjust structures of society are changed into structures of grace. (Lambeth Conference, 1988, sections 1 and 8e)

So the mission of God comes through the saving, serving and liberating work of Christ in the power of the Spirit. And its purpose is the coming of the kingdom of God's glory. To borrow Hans Küng's phrase: 'God's kingdom is creation healed' (Küng, 1977, p. 231). God's mission is about the healing of creation and the fulfilment of all humanity in Christ. As Irenaeus put it, 'The glory of God is a human being fully alive.'

The gospel is not primarily about the Church. Jesus Christ came to call people into the kingdom of God's glory, that is the healing of all creation, and the coming fully alive of all humanity. The Church and its mission are a means to that end – and indeed to the End of all things in God's purposes, in which all existence fully bears witness to God.

So when we talk about the mission of the Church in today's world, we need to be speaking about the ways in which the Christian Church is being caught up into the mission of God, the ways in which we discern God at work ahead of us in the world, and the ways in which we are being made part of his work of saving, serving and liberating. The mission of the Church is thus part of that outflowing, centrifugal movement of the love of God for the growth of the kingdom of God's glory, in which all of creation is made whole and people come fully alive.

Mission is more than evangelism. By 'evangelism' I mean

that aspect of mission which consciously extends (by presence or proclamation) an invitation to those outside the faith to share in the life of the kingdom of God, and seeks for a response. Mission is broader and wider than evangelism. Nor has mission much to do with marquees and crooning choirs. Nor with getting people to come to church. It is much more about the Church taking its doors off their hinges so that something of God's saving, serving and liberating love can flow out. Clearly it is a good thing if people do want to come in. It is a good thing if more and more people want to join together in the worship of God. The vision of the kingdom of God's glory is of a community of people of all tribes and families and nations and languages sharing together in the worship of God. There is an important 'coming in'. But the primary movement of mission is not getting people in, but being part of the love of God reaching out, and connecting the gospel of God's love with all the messy and muddled dimensions of our economic, social, political and personal lives. It is then that 'the Lord adds to the Church daily those who are being saved' (cf. Acts 2.47). Mission is thus a broad and wide-ranging task. It is not the whole task of the Church, which is primarily to worship God and give ourselves and our work and our lives to him. Mission is offering ourselves and our work and our lives in the service of God's world and God's people. So worship and mission belong inseparably together.

The Church's mission, then, is personal and social, not restricted to individual choices, but also including the wider communities in which people live their lives. It is local and global, concerned both with small-scale questions of justice and liberation, and with the care of the whole of the created order of which God calls us to be stewards. Mission is private and public – covering the intimate attitudes of the human heart in the secret of a person's own conscience and character, and also the public truth of social attitudes, cultural values and the structures of human communities. It touches the intellect and the emotions: is addressed to the mind as well as the heart. It is proclamation and presence – the work of the Spirit in proclaiming the Word, and the work of the Spirit in mediating

God's presence. It is a reaching out more than a pulling in – it is being caught up into the mission of God.

Mission in our changing world

The Church has not, of course, always understood mission in exactly the same way.[3] Christians in the past have found ways of building bridges between the gospel and their cultures, making links between mission and worship, the development of character, the health of their communities, and the political situations in which they found themselves. The question for us is, 'What does mission mean for our day?' How do we learn from the mission themes of the past to build bridges to our contemporary culture for the gospel? To engage creatively with the wider political society? To make links between worship, liturgy, art, the development of Christian character, individual vocation, and the mission of the Church? What do we need to be doing to be sharing in the saving, serving and liberating work of Christ for the world in which God has given us the chance to live? How do we pray and work for the coming of the Kingdom which is creation healed? How do we as the Church of Jesus Christ become the servant of others, so that they and we can become more fully alive?

Assumptions

Some years ago, church buildings often displayed posters called The Wayside Pulpit – a text from the Bible attractively presented for passers-by to read. One of the most popular was the text from John 3.16 which we have already quoted: 'God so loved the world that he gave his only Son, that whoever believes in him should not perish but have eternal life.' That is the text I have chosen as the basis for the chapters which follow. These chapters will not be a detailed exposition of the text; rather I will use the phrases of the text as a series of pegs on which to hang discussion of many of the diverse aspects of mission.

This text, which speaks of God, of his love for the world, of his Son, of believing in him, of perishing and of having everlasting life, clearly makes a large number of assumptions which many people living in the contemporary world do not share. Indeed many of the aspects of modernity and post-modernity throw into very sharp relief a large number of the assumptions on which the Christian gospel is based. In the rest of this chapter we will unpack some of these theological assumptions, and then – phrase by phrase – briefly indicate how these assumptions have been questioned throughout the period of modernity and more recently. We will relate this discussion to the five key themes we mentioned earlier: ideology, moral understanding, patterns of social life, rationality, and the idea of progress. They will then be part of our agenda for later chapters.

An agenda for this book

Ideology

To start with, to speak of God is to make an ideological assumption about theism. Theism is the belief that there is a foundation to all being, thought, morality and significance in a personal God. Christian theism tells a 'big story' about the world in relation to God as Creator, Law Giver, Redeemer and Reconciler, Lover, Shepherd, Father and King – a story within which the smaller stories of human cultures, and the intimate stories of people's lives can then be understood to find their meaning and significance. To use the jargon, this is an over-arching 'metanarrative' with a larger basis for human knowing and being than anything else.

This theistic ideology gave place during the period of modernity to other 'big stories', associated with names like Newton (the world is a machine), Darwin (the world is an evolving organism), Marx (the big story is dialectical materialism), Freud (life is rooted in biological instincts). The Christian story no longer held sway as the 'big story' by which everything else was interpreted.

But for many who describe themselves as post-modern, there simply are no 'big stories' any more. There are, they say, no metanarratives. There is no shared meaning. We all simply create our meanings for ourselves. In art, post-modernity is expressed in pastiche, in montage, in collage, in the spontaneity of a Jackson Pollock canvas. Everything is a collection of bits and pieces; there is no standard by which to measure them; their meaning arises from what they are. In literature and popular culture, post-modernity is often expressed in terms of the loss of meaning. Developing the view of Nietzsche that 'all that exists consists of *interpretations*', others indicate that there is no meaning beyond language. Language no longer refers beyond itself to something in the real world; there is only language and interpretation, and interpretations of interpretations. All language then floats freely, severed from connections with the world. Language can only be understood at all in relation to other language. As David Lyon put it: 'Like ice-floes on the river during spring break-up, the world of meaning fractures into fragments, making it hard even to speak of meaning as traditionally conceived' (Lyon, 1994).

Can our mission recover a sense that faith in the living God is meaningful? Clearly if the Christian faith is to recover its nerve about the 'big story' of the Word of God becoming flesh in Jesus, we are going to have to engage with some of these enormous changes in ideology, and the ways our culture thinks about meanings. I want to argue that a recovery of the sense of God is not only possible, but makes very good sense of much of our ordinary human experience.

Moral understanding

To say that God 'so loved that he gave' is to make a statement about demonstrated love. We are talking about God's love for the world, whether we recognize it or not – and therefore about an objective moral order.

However, modernity has emphasized subjectivity in morality, which has led to the general tolerance of many different viewpoints – moral pluralism. The reactions to the end of modernity have been twofold: some writers within post-modernity celebrate variety, heterogeneity and difference, and celebrate the demise of the concept of moral truth, welcoming instead the chaos of moral relativism. But significantly, there are others who are moving back towards the possibilities and need for a shared morality in which something objective can be held on to as the basis for social life – what Iris Murdoch called 'deep foundations'.

If Christian faith is to speak about a God who 'so loved that he gave', we are going to find ourselves in dialogue with those for whom morality is a question only of relative truth and subjective decision. I believe that part of Christian mission will be to demonstrate love in action through self-giving service, and through its social expression – justice – in the world, in the context of pluralism and variety.

Social patterns
When we use the language of 'God's Son', we are drawn into the complicated theological concept of God as a Holy Trinity of Persons in relationship. And if, as Christian faith affirms, we humans are made in the image of this God, then interpersonal relating and communion are essentially what being human is about. And yet one of the features of modernity is the stress on the individual. In both individualism and in its mirror image, collectivism, I believe we see a loss of 'the personal' in the way Christians have understood it.

In social terms, modernity is linked to the growth of avowedly democratic forms of political life, coupled with a growing Western imperialism. Modernity takes form within certain institutions, for example a capitalist economy, separation of powers in government, the separation of church and state, the privatization of aspects of social life, the growth of bureaucracy. The results of this can be seen in town planning, which became increasingly geared to production, rapid transport and social mobility. The 'technical' solution to concentrations of workforce, and the need to keep work and leisure (green belt) separate, was the high-rise flats, with increased atomization, depersonalization and alienation. The gradual loss of the personal (as an organic network of interpersonal relationships) contributed to the growth of individualism – which came to its high point in the Thatcherite 'There is no such thing as society.' It also contributed to the growth of totalitarian collectivism, which ideologically sought to confront the alienation of workers from leaders, but in fact crushed the personal into an undifferentiated state.

The priority of the individual over the community, coupled with increasing cultural splits between public and private worlds, reason and emotion, mind and body, facts and values, led to deep cultural fissures down which words like 'society', 'community' and 'fellowship' could fall. The city became a collection of many individuals whose working lives were separated from their home lives, whose leisure was separated from their families, whose religious life had no impact on the rest of their lives, whose work was separated from the products – in short, in Marxist terms, a context of alienation.

Many of the reactions of post-modernity show that often social organizations, even those set up for the welfare of the individual, in fact disempower persons. Around 1900, Max Weber suggested that the coming together of instrumental reason with growing bureaucracy would lead to an 'iron cage' of oppressive, scientifically programmed society and the dictatorship of bureaucrats. However, once again, some writers are recovering the language of organism, interconnectedness and belonging to the whole. I want to explore how Christian mission can recover the value of community.

Rationality

When John's Gospel refers to 'believing in', the writer is using the language of commitment. The sense of the phrase he uses is really 'belief into'. But commitment to anything or to anyone is not something that comes easily, or indeed makes much sense, in a culture that has forgotten how to develop the capacity to make commitments.

Through the developments of modernity, science, the quest for truth – for what Kepler called 'thinking God's thoughts after him' – became superseded by a commitment to 'instrumental reason', that is the priority of technique, the gradual fusion of science and technology, and the growth of a technological mind-set which believed that by asking the right questions, and by technical intervention, human beings would inevitably find the right answers, and improve their world. Industrialization, concentration on production, and urbanization, are the result of the growth of technology, and it is unarguable that there has been enormous benefit to humanity through this achievement. We are now, however, also taking stock of the environmental costs of some industrial progress.

Some commentators on modernity, such as Jürgen Habermas, are trying to hold on to the positive values of the Enlightenment, but also to return to a more broad, practical and positive view of human reason than that which we have described as instrumental reason. But inevitably for some others, there is a reaction more of despair and meaninglessness. The whole basis of the Enlightenment project is rejected, leading for some writers to a denial of rationality, and to the realization of Nietzsche's nihilistic vision of a world in which God is dead.

Our missionary theology will need to engage with contemporary questions about rationality.

Purpose and the idea of progress
The language of our text, of 'perishing' and the hope of 'eternal life', reflects an assumption that the world is going somewhere, there is a direction to our history, that it makes sense to talk about purpose. All things, Christians believed, were held by the Providence of God. But 'purpose' is a word which is regarded by many today as meaningless; things just are, and to seek for deeper meanings and purposes is to seek for fantasy.

Modernity was coupled with an overriding belief in progress – at least until the First World War. Trust in Providence gave way to the idea of Progress. This commitment to progress, linked in some people's minds to Darwinian evolutionism, and the priority of survival – and the sense that all problems are in principle solvable – was coupled with a rejection of divine causality behind all things, and the rejection of any concept of purpose.

Modernity's rejection of Providence in favour of Progress has led to nihilism, the rejection of the category of purpose, and increasing social alienation. Some of the negative aspects of post-modernity invite us to embrace the void and the chaos, and abandon hope. Others see the transformations of post-modernity as new opportunities to recover or rediscover a sense of meaning. Part of the mission of the Christian Church, I want to argue, is to be a bearer of meaning, significance and hope.

How does the Christian Church go about its mission? Do we do this through Christian presence, Christian political action, Christian proclamation? I am sure it has to do with all these, in which many different elements of mission belong together. Among these I want to list: worship, apologetics, religious experience, demonstrated love, social justice, the creation of community, the recovery of the capacity for commitment. These are the themes which will set our agenda.

There is, of course, much more to Christianity, to modernity and to post-modernity than the sketches in this book suggest. But modernity and post-modernity put questions to Christian faith which any understanding of Christian mission must take very seriously. And it is in this contemporary context that the Christian Church must bear its witness and offer its service.

The table (on page 19) sets out in simplified form some of the themes of this chapter.

1 The first column identifies the headings, taken from John 3.16, which will form the basis of discussion in later chapters of this book.
2 The column headed 'Theology' offers corresponding theological themes, and the five headings used for our agenda: ideology, morality, social patterns, rationality and purpose.
3 The 'Modernity' column indicates some of the responses of the Enlightenment philosophy to these traditional theological themes. In place of a theistic story, other non-theistic stories were told (Newton, Darwin, Marx etc.). In place of a

Outline of themes presented in this chapter

	Theology	Modernity	Post-modernity (and other responses to modernity)
God ...	theistic foundation: the overarching big story (metanarrative) = *ideology*	non-theistic foundations: other metanarratives (e.g. Newton, Darwin, Marx, Freud)	*either:* incredulity towards all metanarratives *or:* recovery of the sense of God
so loved that he gave ...	the objectivity of demonstrated love = *morality*	moral values become matters of subjective choice	*either:* moral relativism *or:* recovery of Value
his only Son ...	persons-in-relation = *social patterns*	the emphasis on the individual *and the corresponding loss of* the person-in-relation – either in individualism or totalitarianism	*either:* *the iron cage of bureaucracy* *or:* recovery of wholism
that whoever believes in him ...	faith as commitment and participation = *rationality*	the priority of instrumental reason; the loss of creativity; the stress on the importance of technique	*either:* denial of rationality *or:* broadening out of rationality
should not perish, but have eternal life.	redemption, overcoming alienation; the gift of purpose and offer of hope = *purpose*	belief in human progress; but a rejection of final causes and loss of purpose	*either:* embrace the void with despair *or:* recover sense of meaning, purpose and hope

belief in the objectivity of morality, moral values become matters of subjective choice. The growth of individualism (and totalitarianism) replaces a social understanding of the personal. The Enlightenment opened up the road to an emphasis on 'instrumental reason' which replaced a broader conception of reason related to faith. Belief in human progress took the place of faith in providence and in the purposes of God.

4 The column 'Post-modernity' indicates some of the responses of contemporary thinkers to modernity. Some of the reactions are negative (*'either:'*). These more negative reactions tend to be brought under the heading of 'Post-modernity'. Others – at least from a Christian point of view – are more positive (*'or:'*), though many of these responses to modernity might not be comfortable being labelled 'post-modern'.

The book explores some of these themes in more detail:

- Chapters 1 and 2 consider the reality of God – responding to some of the questions of ideology, and Chapter 3 discusses 'the world' as the object of God's love.
- Chapter 4 picks up the questions of morality.
- Chapter 5 explores the meaning of persons-in-relation and links this with our discussion of social patterns.
- Chapter 6 provides an opportunity to take further the discussion of rationality.
- Chapter 7 looks broadly at questions of purpose and hope in the light of the meaning of forgiveness.

Throughout we shall be asking what implications our discussion has for Christian mission – and will draw the threads together in Chapter 8.

Chapter 1

GLIMPSES OF GOD

To speak of God, we said, is to make an ideological assumption about theism – the belief that there is a foundation to all being, thought, morality and significance in a personal God. Christian theism tells a 'big story' about the world in relation to the God who is made known in Jesus Christ – a metanarrative which overarches all other stories and which provides a larger basis for human knowing and being than anything else.

But how do we know God exists? If we are looking for a logical proof, we will be disappointed. God is not the end of a syllogism. There have been times in the history of Christian theology when people have talked about proofs for the existence of God. They have based these arguments on philosophical discussions about the nature of Being, or the need for a First Cause, on the discovery of what looks like 'design' in the world, on the fact that as human beings we find ourselves faced with moral obligations, on the widespread reality of religious experience. Most of these arguments in a strictly logical sense add up to nothing very much. It would be rather puzzling if they did. If God is discovered as the end of a syllogism, or if God is necessary to make a philosophical argument hold water, he is not the God of Christian faith. As the philosopher Blaise Pascal discovered, the hidden God who confronted him in Jesus Christ on 23 November 1654 was someone other than the God who served merely as the end of a philosophical argument. He wrote of his experience on a piece of parchment found sewn into his coat after his death:

Fire
'God of Abraham, God of Isaac, God of Jacob', not of philosophers and scholars.

Certainty, certainty, heartfelt joy, peace.
God of Jesus Christ.
God of Jesus Christ.
My God and your God ...

Although the traditional Arguments for the existence of God –
the Argument from causality, the Argument from religious
experience, the Moral Argument, the Argument from design,
and so on – add up to a logical zero, they did, in their own
ways, nonetheless demonstrate that faith in the God and
Father of Jesus Christ was a reasonable faith to hold in the
light of contemporary knowledge. Some of the discussion of this
book picks up and adapts some of these traditional themes.
There are reminders of the traditional Argument from
Religious Experience in Chapter 2. There are echoes of the
Argument from Design in Chapter 3, when we discuss contemporary science. There are hints of the traditional Moral
Argument in Chapter 4. They are not offered as proofs of the
existence of God – more as buttresses to support the conviction
that faith in God is reasonable.

In this chapter I want to set out my stall more broadly,
suggesting that there are many aspects of ordinary human life
which point beyond themselves to the reality of God. In
particular, I focus on two: our experience of beauty, and our
experience of death.

Pointing beyond

I enjoy watching snooker on television. I did even in the days
before we could afford a colour television set – which made for
some problems, not greatly helped by the commentator who
once famously said, 'For those of you watching in black and
white, the pink is the one behind the green.'

However, what watching the snooker balls in various shades
of grey on a black and white set did was demonstrate that
'there must be more than this'. What I could see and
experience pointed beyond itself to other aspects of reality

which I could not see, but whose assumed reality made sense of what I could. There were signals, hints, pointers, at the level of black and white which suggested that there must be much more to this game if I could see it in all the variety of its true colours. It is that sense of 'pointing beyond' that is the concern of this chapter.

An even better analogy was provided when we did get a colour set, but had not tuned it properly. Then the picture was still mostly black and white, but just occasionally there were flickering glimpses of colour which showed the picture in all its true, but mostly hidden, glory!

In 1969 Peter Berger wrote a book called *A Rumour of Angels* in which he explored various observable features of ordinary human experience and interpreted them as 'signals of transcendence' by which he meant 'pointers toward a religious interpretation of the human situation' (pp. 70, 81). Many common human experiences, he argues, can be interpreted as pointing beyond themselves to a deeper reality of order, love or goodness which can give meaning to them. He writes, for example, about our human quest for order, our deep experiences of love or sorrow, our moral sense – particularly moral outrage at something we can only name as 'evil' – and the widespread denial of death. In this and later chapters in this book we will discuss some of these experiences in more detail.

Although I am very attracted by the phrase 'signals of transcendence', I have a hesitation. In some people's minds 'transcendence' has come to mean 'distance'. In one of Helmut Thielicke's sermons he speaks of the way the 'lofty God' is sometimes made unreachable, out of touch with ordinary life:

Tell me how lofty God is for you, and I'll tell you how little he means to you. That could be a theological axiom. The lofty God has been lofted right out of my private life.

It is certainly remarkable but it is true. God has become of concern to me only because he has made himself *smaller* than the Milky Way, only because he is present in my little sickroom when I gasp for breath, or understands the little cares I cast on him ... He concerns me because Jesus Christ takes my speck of anxiety and my personal guilt upon himself. (Thielicke, 1969, p. 33)

The heart of Christian faith is that God is not only transcendent, but intimately involved in, incarnated within, the ordinarinesses of our world – the world of science, of poverty, of war, of sickness and of joy, of beauty and of ugliness, of politics and personal intimacies. Archbishop William Temple wrote of both 'the transcendence of the immanent' and 'the immanence of the transcendent' (chapter headings in Temple, 1934). If God is of significance, that significance is to be found not only in majestic distance, but primarily also in the small mosaic-pieces of our lives. It is God's presence, rather than his distance, that I wish to be able to stress: what George Herbert called 'heaven in ordinary' (Herbert, 1981, 'Prayer' I).

So I hesitate over Berger's phrase, 'signals of transcendence', if that can sometimes be taken to mean that to find God we have to look above our ordinary experience to some higher realm or higher reality. Although God is majestically transcendent over all things as creator and sovereign, it is in and through the 'flesh' which the Word became that we most clearly hear God speak. It is in and through the paint and the canvas that we see the picture.

So I accept Peter Berger's description: 'pointers toward a religious interpretation of the human situation'. And although I shall sometimes borrow his phrase, 'signals of transcendence', I shall at other times prefer to speak of 'glimpses of God' – those moments in our ordinary lives when the ordinariness points beyond itself to some deeper reality which is always there but not always seen, not always heard.

For a long time in Western civilization the deeper reality which gave meaning to human life and experience was God. It was to God that the early scientists looked as they sought to 'think God's thoughts after him' in their exploration of the order of the world. The correspondence between the rationality of their minds and the rational order they discovered in the world of their experiments was possible, they thought, because

God the creator made the world and also made human beings in his image, capable of rational thought.

It was to God that moral theologians looked to provide a basis for human morality, a transcendent source of goodness which gave human beings criteria for deciding on good and bad, right and wrong, because human beings were made in the image of a God who is good.

It was to God that the authors of the Christian marriage service looked, as they understood that the mutual love and commitment of husband and wife reflected in some way the love and commitment made by God to his people, Christ to his Church. The love of God was experienced in human loving, because human beings were made in the image of the God of love.

Furthermore, for a long time, the reality of spiritual experience, expressed in worship, prayer, contemplation, awe in the face of mystery, was also interpreted in terms of a living relationship between human beings and God their creator and redeemer. Religious experience was not simply a private matter of personal temperament and taste: people believed themselves to be in touch with the Spirit of the living God who was there.

In Europe, the predominant story up until the time of the Enlightenment that was told about the rationality, order, goodness and love of God, and of the possibility of human beings coming into touch with the life of God, was the Christian story.

The Christian story is grounded in the conviction that God is. But we need to say more than that, because the Christian story is more than a vague deism or even theism – it starts from the fact that the Christian meaning of the term 'God' is essentially related two ways (cf. Webster, 1995). It is related to Jesus Christ as the embodiment in our world's history, within this world's time and space, of God's own being, saving will and activity. It is related also to the present life-giving and life-sustaining energy of God in the world, described as the 'Holy Spirit'. In other words, the Christian story tells us, God is intrinsically relational: at the heart of this universe is a

God who is interpersonal communion, who is – in God's own
self – relationships of love, freedom and communication, and
from whom all life, personhood and creativity derives. God is
Trinity – an essential relation of God the creator of all things,
from whom all things exist (God the Father), God the
redeemer of all things, in whom all things come to their
fulfilment (God the Son), and God the life-giver and sanctifier
(Holy Spirit), in whom all things have their life, energy and
joy, and are transformed and re-ordered towards the purposes
which God has for the whole of creation – that is the kingdom
of his glory.

The Christian story, then, is rooted in history in the life and
teaching, death and resurrection of Jesus Christ, and a story
continually re-energized and re-enacted in the world, and
especially within the sacramental and worshipping life of the
Christian Church, through the power of the Holy Spirit.

Signals of transcendence and glimpses of God

We turn now to consider some of the signals which, we may
believe, point towards God, and towards the reasonableness of
the Christian story, some of the glimpses of God which sometimes we see. Alongside the signals provided by religious
experience, by science and by morality (which we discuss in
later chapters), and supremely in Jesus Christ – the one whom
Irenaeus referred to as being 'fully alive' – there are many
aspects of our human experience in this world which point
beyond themselves.

The child psychoanalyst D. W. Winnicott (1974) describes
how every individual not only operates to some extent with
both an 'inner world' and an 'outer world' but also with an
'intermediate' area of experience to which both inner thoughts
and feelings and outer circumstances contribute. His classic
observation of infant development is that some thing may
emerge for a baby, especially at a time of anxiety such as
going to sleep, some thing which is very important to the

baby – a bundle of wool, a mannerism, a tune, a special blanket, a teddy bear. This 'transitional object' occupies the intermediate territory of that child between their inner and outer worlds.

In adult life, that transitional phenomenon still exists, but instead (usually) of the teddy bear, the intermediate experience is one of play, artistic creativity, religious feeling, ritual and so on. In a mature person, the transitional sphere mediates between external and internal worlds, and enables the appreciation of beauty, of art, music and religious ritual. It is perhaps in that transitional sphere that experiences of God are best understood – though more like a work of art than a teddy bear! Clearly the transitional sphere can sometimes fall apart – it can dissolve into mere fantasy and illusion in my mind on the one hand, or mere external ritual on the other. But if Winnicott is correct, in the mature adult the experiences we all know as experiences of beauty, of wonder, of appreciation of meaning without words, are best understood within this transitional personal space.

The psychologists Fraser Watts and Mark Williams build on Winnicott's view of the significance of play and trust in infant development, and of the growth and change in a person's mental life as they mature. They comment:

> It is in this transitional world ... that ... the representation of God is created for the individual. In Prusyer's striking words, 'the transitional object is the transcendent' ... The representation of God is rich enough to allow continual re-working and renewal. Perhaps more than any other representation in the transitional sphere, God is uniquely and powerfully related to man's sense of himself and his destiny. The world in which God is experienced is a world of 'play' and 'trust' in which man can come to understand both himself and external reality. (Watts and Williams, 1988, pp. 35f.)

Of course the world in which a child grows, the world all adults experience, is one of ambiguity. There is destructiveness as well as creativity, ugliness as well as beauty, despair as well as joy. But the fact that suffering, ugliness and despair are problems to us, rather than simply just one of those things, is itself a pointer to the fact that we have concepts of health, beauty and joy against which to measure them. And the fact that there is also creativity, beauty and joy in the world – and that it is these which evoke in most of us our deepest feelings of satisfaction, belonging, of being held in a universe that is ultimately 'on our side', of awe, of wonder, of worship – this also points beyond to a transcendent reality within which we have our being, and which Christian faith describes in terms of the reality of God.

I have chosen two examples to illustrate what I mean: beauty and death.

Beauty

Simone Weil (1977) writes much about beauty when she is discussing 'forms of the implicit love of God'. Beauty, she says, is 'eternity here below' (p. 96). 'The beauty of the world is Christ's tender smile for us coming through matter' (p. 97). 'A sense of beauty, although mutilated, distorted and soiled, remains rooted in the heart of man as a powerful incentive ... the beauty of the world is the commonest, easiest and most natural way of approach [to the feet of God] (p. 101). By 'beauty', of course, Weil does not merely mean 'prettiness' (to borrow a comment from Harries, 1993). What matters to her is that order, truth and integrity point towards God, and it is the purity of these which is beauty.

We might think first of music. Where *is* the music when I attend a concert? Not wholly in my head, and not wholly in the outer world. 'Music arises in my soul when I am reminded by the instruments.' Music conveys meaning without the necessary use of words.

P. T. Forsyth links the power of music very closely to spirituality:

When the visibility of the picture passes into the audibility of music, we call into play a sense more spiritual than sight, and one which better suits the recipient and often passive attitude of the soul in the hour of spiritual revelation.

There is a vaster power in music than in any other art of entering sympathetically into the shades and varieties of emotion, and this sets up a very close bond between the musician and his varied audience, and enables him, as it were, to pour his soul directly into theirs, duly dividing the word of power in flame that flickers on every head. And in worship, it gives a facility for the common spiritual expression of unutterable things ... (Forsyth, 1911, pp. 192ff.)

Bach's music, in particular, was written to be participated in as part of the worship of the Church. It was a ministry of the Word – for Bach, as Robin Leaver (1981) put it, music was preaching.

The theologian Karl Barth writes about 'the incomparable' Mozart, who was composing at the time of the massive Lisbon earthquake, when many were questioning the providence of God:

He knew something about creation in its total goodness ... He had heard, and causes those who have ears to hear ... what we shall not see until the end of time – the whole context of providence. As though in the light of this end, he heard the harmony of creation to which the shadow also belongs but in which the shadow is not darkness, deficiency is not defeat, sadness cannot become despair, trouble cannot degenerate into tragedy ... the light shines all the more brightly because it breaks forth from the shadow ... Mozart saw this light no more than we do, but he heard the whole world of creation enveloped by this light ... He simply offered himself as the agent by which little bits of horn, metal and catgut could serve as the voices of creation. (Barth, 1956–75, vol. III. 1, p. 298)

Michael Mayne, formerly Dean of Westminster, whose beautiful letters to his godchildren in *This Sunrise of Wonder* (1995) uncover his delight in the natural world as well as in literature and art, also finds an expression of wonder through music. He quotes Hans Küng's comment that for him the music of Mozart reveals 'how wafer-thin is the boundary between the human and the divine':

> To listen to the adagio of the Clarinet Concerto, for ex-ample, is to perceive something wholly other: the sound of an infinite which transcends us and for which 'beauty' is no description ... To describe such experience and revelation of transcendence, religious language still needs the word God. (Mayne, 1995, quoting Küng, 1992, p. 34)

Music can give a rich glimpse of the beauty of God.

And so can the visual arts. Richard Harries says boldly, 'All works of art, whatever their content, have a spiritual dimension'.[1] His view is based, like Weil's, on the conviction that, even when art is dealing with terrible themes, they can nonetheless convey truth and reality, and when those themes are expressed in a 'form' or an 'order' they can be described as 'beauty'. The reason is, he argues, that all form derives ultimately from the order of God's world in the Logos; all beauty points to the beauty of God. Art engages with us, and serves as what I have called a glimpse of God, because it arouses within us, and to some extent answers to, some deep longing within the human heart. He puts it this way:

> This desire for communion with the inexpressibly lovely is ... only part of the reason for the intensity of longing aroused by experiences of beauty. The other part is the deep desire that we ourselves might be changed so that this beauty becomes part of us, that we become what we behold. (Harries, 1993, p. 95)

Of the vast field of visual arts, there is space here for only one example. Why is it that on any given afternoon in the Musée de l'Orangerie in Paris, there will be a few dozen people sitting, sometimes for a considerable time, in front of Claude Monet's massive *Nymphéas – Water-lilies* (cf. Pattison, 1991, p. 149)? Or why will there be a few scores of people queuing to visit Monet's garden in Giverny, where the lake with the water-lilies may be seen? Despite the criticisms sometimes levelled at the French impressionists that they were concerned only with the surface of things, only with the effects of colour and of light, there is in Monet's series of paintings

> an infinity of forms and shades, the complex life of things ... Then each picture would become a world of its own, one of those summaries of a moment in which the impressionism of Claude Monet could express the universal. (Gregoire, 1994, quoting Geffroy, 1922)

George Pattison's comments on Monet seem appropriate:

> These paintings assure us, in an irreducibly pictorial way, that the world is a good place to be, that it is holy ground, that we may trust ourselves to the particularity of our carnal situatedness and find in it a texture of meaning and value of the first order. (Pattison, 1991, p. 149)

We also have experiences of beauty in the natural world. To stand on the high road overlooking the great gorges and waterfalls in the Yosemite National Park, to fly over the Grand Canyon, to look at a snow-covered mountain peak, to watch the sun going down over a Scottish loch, to be alone in the dark under a clear starry sky – these can give us glimpses of glory.[2]

As Thomas Traherne wrote in the seventeenth century:

> It is a natural effect of infinite Wisdome to make every of its Treasures suitable to its own excellence. And that the Wisdome of God has done, by asking the smallest Thing in his Kingdome infinitely serviceable in its Place and Station, for the manifesting of his Wisdome, Goodness and Glory to the Eye of a clear Beholder ... Relating to all the innumerable Parts, receiving a Beauty from all, and communicating

a Beauty to all, even to all objects throughout all Eternity.
(Dowell, 1990, p. 55, quoting Traherne, 1675)

The same thought is picked up by Gerard Manley Hopkins in
'God's Grandeur':

The world is charged with the grandeur of God.

Hopkins coined the word 'inscape' for that collection of data
presented to our senses which together make up the rich
'oneness' of things in the natural world. About 'God's
Grandeur' he writes: 'I thought how sadly beauty of inscape
was unknown and buried away from simple people and yet
how near at hand it was if they had eyes to see it and it could
be called out everywhere again' (Gardner, 1970, p. xxi).

Experiences of beauty function for many of us as 'signals of
transcendence'. These signals are interpreted by Patrick Sherry
in this way in his study *Spirit and Beauty*:

> The divine beauty is to be explained in Trinitarian terms, for
> the Father's glory is reflected in the Son, his perfect image,
> and diffused through the Holy Spirit; ... the Spirit has the
> mission of communicating God's beauty to the world, both
> through creation, in the case of natural beauty, and through
> inspiration, in that of artistic beauty; ... earthly beauty is
> thus a reflection of divine glory and a sign of the way in
> which the Spirit is perfecting creation; ... beauty ... is an
> anticipation of the restored and transfigured world which
> will be the fullness of God's kingdom. (Sherry, 1992, p. 176)

Death

A rather different example of a glimpse of God is death. Given
the low rate of church attendance in Britain, it is perhaps
surprising that a very high proportion of those who die have a
Christian funeral. This is for some people partly because of the
memory of a folk religion; for others there is a long-established
custom of associating ritual mourning with a religious service.

But for many who would never otherwise attend a church, it is still thought important and appropriate for a priest to conduct the proceedings at a cemetery or crematorium. There seems to be more in this than custom, however. A survey carried out some years ago suggested that the word 'death' made 64 per cent of respondents think about God. It also indicated that a much higher proportion of people said they would talk to a clergyman if they were afraid of death than would talk to their doctor. In 1975 Argyle and Beit-Hallahmi offered this comment on some of their research studies in the social psychology of religion, which I believe still has a significant measure of truth: 'It looks as if in Britain today, religion is seen by many people primarily as a means of dealing with death' (see Argyle and Beit-Hallahmi, 1975, pp. 55ff.). There is even now a widespread belief that death is somehow part of the clergyman's job!

In his classic *Rites of Passage* (1960), Arnold Van Gennep gave an account of the way social groups, whether secular or religious, tend to develop various rituals to help individuals cope with life crises and transitions. A ritual helps a person to interpret the changes that are happening. It helps focus the choices that are now open. It helps make the move from one phase of life to another. Funerals can exercise these functions for the bereaved. The importance of appropriate ritual mourning to enable bereaved people to handle their grief in a way that is constructive and healthy is acknowledged by most psychologists and therapists.

Despite what we constantly hear about the 'naturalness' of death, and the fact that we know in our minds that death will come to us all; despite the ways in which modern terminal care can ease – sometimes even sanitize – death; despite the breaking down of some social taboos which used to make aspects of death and dying unacceptable for conversation; despite the way the soft curtains and soft music at the crematorium attempt to take away the pain of loss; most of us still know that something very powerful, rather awesome, sometimes fearful, often deeply painful, is going on when a person close to us dies. It is not only the absence of the friend, in whatever multiplicity of roles we knew them; it is not only the fact of suffering and decay in a person who may have hitherto been full of vitality and joy; it is not only the reminder that we too will die. It is the fact that death itself, we know, is both an end and not an end. We are face to face with the edge of our existence; that which we have known is no more, and we are face to face with mystery. For every philosopher like Bertrand Russell, who affirmed 'I believe that when I die I rot', there are a hundred who simply cannot believe death is just an end.

One of Peter Berger's illustrations of a 'signal of transcendence' refers to those

> observable phenomena of the human situation whose intrinsic intention appears to be a depreciation or even denial of the reality of death ... It would seem ... that both psychologically (in the failure to imagine his own death) and morally (in his violent denial of the death of others) a 'no!' to death is profoundly rooted in the very being of man. (Berger, 1969, p. 81)

The psychologist Lily Pincus (1976) writes of the effect of death in a family in terms of 'the general conspiracy that death has not occurred'. What Becker calls, in his book of that title, *The Denial of Death* (1973), can be interpreted – I would say can best be interpreted – in the light of the faith that there is a God who is not only creator but judge, the giver of life and death.

It is that ambiguity that needs explaining, that death is in one sense the most natural and in another the most unnatural of events (cf. Thielicke, 1983). Christian faith links both sides of the puzzle to the God who is both life-giver and judge. On the one hand, a strand of biblical thought suggests that death is the way it is with living things in this world. 'There is a time to be born and a time to die' (cf. Ecclesiastes 3.1–2; Joshua 23.14; 1 Kings 2.2). Earlier generations made much more of 'preparing for a good death'[3] than would be widely acceptable today.[4] However, there is an 'unnaturalness' to death which contributes to widespread human awe, even fear. As Barth puts it, 'The time we shall then have will be a time with a present (and with our whole past behind us), but with no future ... though we still are, we shall be no longer' (Barth, 1956–75, vol. III.2, p. 589).

Death faces us with the edge of our existence in this world. 'In the midst of life we are in death'.[5] Because our time is finite, our time is therefore, whether we are conscious of it or not, overshadowed by death. What meaning can be given, then, to the fact that our existence in time – our natural life – comes so unnaturally to an end? As Becker (1973) put it, 'the idea of death, the fear of it, haunts the human animal like nothing else: it is the mainspring of human activity – activity designed to avoid death – to overcome it by denying it'.

But where does this fear come from if death is 'only natural'? Another strand of biblical writing speaks of death as a symbol of divine judgement. When God said to the man in the Garden 'When you eat of it you will surely die' (Genesis 2.17), the implication is that death is the divine judgement on human sin. For Adam in the Garden, death was not the end of physical life, it was a change of situation before God. The biblical imagery, of cherubim with flaming swords guarding the way back into the Garden, foreshadows the way in which, in later biblical writings, death becomes a power which can dominate the lives of people and hold humankind in thrall. Death becomes a symbol of the judgement of God against all that is disordered and ungodly about life. To quote Barth once more:

> The man who fears death, even though he contrives to put a somewhat better face on it, is at least nearer to the truth than the man who does not fear it, or rather pretends that there is no reason why he should do so. Since it is a sign of the divine judgement of human sin and guilt, it is very much to be feared. (Barth, 1956–75, vol. III.2, p. 589)

However, in the ministry of Jesus we see him confronting sickness, disease and death. His snorting indignation at the grave of Lazarus indicates his sense that death is an alien intrusion into the goodness of God's world.[6] Yet paradoxically, Jesus dies and so in himself suffers death as the judgement of

God. In his death and resurrection, this 'last enemy' is overcome. Death, in the death of Christ, is declared to be God's
enemy as well, and God

> treats it as such by placing himself at the side of man in the
> verdict there pronounced, and snatching man from its jaws
> by the death of Jesus for him. It remains for us as a sign of
> divine judgement. We no longer have to suffer the judge-
> ment itself. (Barth, 1956–75, vol. III.2, p. 600)

Christian faith then provides a perspective on the human
experience of the ambiguity of death. There is a negative,
evil and symbolic side to death – even when its power is broken
through the life of the Holy Spirit; there is a positive
acceptance that for the believer, death is transformed into
'falling asleep' in Jesus (1 Thessalonians 4.13). Physical death is
an enemy whose sting is drawn, though in physical experience
we still all die.

In frequent pastoral experience, Christian faith in Jesus
Christ, whose death announces that God is with us in death,
and whose resurrection gives hope that life is once again
made new, is a faith which helps people to die, and therefore
also to live.

We have looked at a few of the signals which point towards the
reality of God. We shall look at others in some more detail in
later chapters. The claim being made is that these function as
signals because they are caught up into a 'big story' about
God's purposes for the world, a story told in the life of Israel
recorded in the Old Testament, in the life and teaching of Jesus
Christ borne witness to in the New Testament, a story
constantly re-enacted in the liturgies and life of the Christian
Church throughout the centuries and throughout the world. In
other words, a story that understands itself as both a witness to
and a response to God's self-revelation.

Part of our mission is to recognize the glimpses of God in our
world, to interpret these in the light of our Christian story, to
demonstrate and celebrate the reality of God, not least through

our worship, and to commend the reasonableness and power of
that story in life and love, justice and community throughout
God's world.

Our next task is to explore in more detail some of the aspects
of our experience of God which are of interest to psychologists
of religion. For religious experience, so it seems to me, is one of
the most widespread and persistent pointers in the world and
across the centuries to the reality of God.

Chapter 2
RELIGIOUS EXPERIENCES

O ne of the classic arguments for God's existence is usually called the 'Argument from Religious Experience'. Sometimes this is expressed in terms of the ways in which people have become convinced of God's reality through visions or dreams, inner voices, mystical feelings or ecstatic experiences. However, the truth values of such claims is often hard to assess: the fact that someone had an experience of a particular sort does not of itself guarantee that their interpretation of that experience is true. Thomas Hobbes famously said that when a man tells him that God has spoken to him in a dream, this is no more than to say he dreamed that God spoke to him (Hobbes, 1651, ch. 32).

However, one fact in our world which does need some explanation is the extremely widespread sense, in most cultures, in most of recorded human history, of a spiritual power greater than human which affects us for good or ill, and to which the appropriate response is worship. One fact which needs some explanation, in other words, is the existence of what many people call 'religious experience' (see Lewis, 1959).

The question is sometimes posed, of course, whether religious experience is merely a psychological prop to help the emotionally weak, or whether such experiences are nothing more than physiological mechanisms in the brain. These questions are part of the agenda for the psychology of religion – a discipline which has been receiving a considerable academic boost in the past two decades, and which it will repay a brief detour to explore. The seriousness with which some contemporary scientists are approaching the reality of religious experience is a helpful antidote to the popular dismissive attitudes of those who keep insisting that religion and science are implacably opposed to each other.

Although this discussion will not provide any proof that all claimed religious experiences are truly experiences of God, and will not provide an unanswerable response to sceptics like Thomas Hobbes, it will suggest that one – perhaps the best – rational explanation for many religious experiences is that they are themselves glimpses of God, signals pointing beyond themselves. It is worthwhile taking a little time to find our bearings.

The psychology of religion

The history of the conversation between theology, religious experience and what we now call psychology, goes back a long way.

In his book *Intimations of Reality*, Arthur Peacocke[1] describes theology in terms of 'the reflective and intellectual analysis of the religious experience of mankind and, in particular, of the Christian experience' (p. 37). These words could easily describe what some of the early Christian thinkers who worked at the interface between theology and what we now call psychology thought they were doing. The development of psychology as a science during the past one hundred years for a while hampered that conversation, though in more recent 'psychology of religion' that conversation has thankfully come alive again.

The interaction and mutual illumination of (what we now call) psychology and theology, has a long history in the Christian tradition. In the third century, Tertullian's *De Anima*, and in the fourth, Augustine's *Confessions* are complex interactions of theological and psychological insights. Thomas Aquinas wrote several treatises on the soul, and one of the major works of the Reformation period was Melanchthon's *Commentarius de Anima*. It was in 1746, however, that 'perhaps the most notable theological attempt to discern the relationship between the inner spiritual life and the more visible and public' was published by the great New England philosopher and theologian, the 'founding father of psychology of religion', Jonathan Edwards, in his *Treatise Concerning Religious Affections*.

Edwards was one of the sources of inspiration, 150 years later, for his fellow New Englander William James, the most famous name in the psychology of religion. By James's time, psychology was practised as a science, and the interaction between psychological and theological insights had significantly declined. It was a tremendous boost to that conversation that a philosopher and psychologist as eminent as William James should give serious attention to religious experience.

It is usual to date the birth of psychology as a science with Wilhelm Wundt's Leipzig laboratory in 1872. We should probably then date the beginnings of the scientific psychological study of religion in 1881 with the publication of G. S. Hall's empirical study of conversion. This was followed by work from J. H. Leuba in 1896, and in 1899 Edwin Starbuck wrote the first systematic study under the title *The Psychology of Religion*. By far the most influential work from that early period was the series of Gifford Lectures given by William James in Edinburgh in 1901–2 and published as *The Varieties of Religious Experience*. For a scholar of James's eminence to explore religious experience gave academic respectability to the idea that a human being's religious nature can be studied like any other aspect of human experience. For James, religion was 'the feelings, acts and experiences of individual men in their solitude, so far as they stand in relation to whatever they may consider the divine' (James, 1952, p. 31). His concern was the solitary individual, especially one whose experience displays an intense and extreme (and therefore to James's mind, the purest) form of religious experience. He drew from a wide variety of biographies, testimonies and anecdotes, and discussed these in terms of 'healthymindedness', 'the sick soul', 'conversion', 'saintliness' and 'mysticism'. He endorsed Jonathan Edwards' major theme that true religion is known 'by its fruits'.

That is not to say that James's approach was universally accepted; there were critics at the time and more recently. In his book *Easter in Ordinary* (1986), for example, Nicholas Lash, though welcoming James's pragmatic question about religion, 'Does it work?', has serious questions about the scope of James's interests. When we ask 'work for whom?' James restricts his attention to 'a small company of creative artists' who testify to some sort of 'mystical experience'. Lash is right to insist that mysticism cannot be analysed down only to religious 'feelings', and, more importantly, that the experience of God is really one way of looking at the general experiences people have in ordinary life. Despite its severe limitations, however, James's *Varieties* had a very significant effect on the intellectual world of the time, and has provided most of the agenda for the on-going psychology of religion.

By the 1920s psychological interest in religious experience began to wane. This may have been partly due to the development of a more positivistic approach to the nature of empirical science, partly to the growth of behaviourism, which had little interest in factors which fell outside the field of observation and measurement, and partly to the movement from the laboratory to the clinician's couch in the work of Sigmund Freud and Carl Gustav Jung.

Freud was fairly hostile to religion, though he did acknowledge that for some people it had therapeutic value. He offered two main theories of the psychological roots of religion, both of which had considerable influence. In *Totem and Taboo* (1913), he proposed that religion represents an elaborate projection of the need to cope with guilt, shame and remorse arising from primitive jealousies. Later, in *The Future of an Illusion*, he saw religion as compensation for frustration and stress provided by a fantasy protective father figure. In neither was there any engagement with theology.

Freud's one-time disciple and younger collaborator, until they went their separate ways, Carl Jung was much more positive towards religion than Freud, believing that a religious attitude was natural to human beings, and associating experiences of God with the unconscious levels of mind which Jung believed all people share. Jung did enter into conversation with many aspects of Christian theology. He even wanted to rewrite some of it.

Freud's and Jung's lesser-known contemporary Ian Suttie in 1935 included a major discussion of religion in his *The Origins of*

Love and Hate, asking whether the parallels between religious teachings and the social development of children throw light on the meaning of the 'supernatural' parts of the Christian tradition. The Object Relations psychologists, as they were called, following on from Suttie and others, have opened up some themes in developmental psychology of considerable interest to theology, for instance in the exploration of guilt, shame, envy, gratitude, creativity and so on.

In 1950 Gordon Allport wrote a small but very influential book, *The Individual and His Religion*. He explored 'the place of religion in the life economy of the individual', and later wrote of the distinction between 'extrinsic' religion (of people who *use* their religion) and 'intrinsic religion' (of people who *live* their religion). He developed various questionnaire techniques to measure these different religious orientations. As a leading American psychologist, he provided another encouragement to experimental psychologists to take an interest in religion. Since then the field has developed increasingly fast. The *Journal for the Scientific Study of Religion* was established in 1962, and there has been an exponential growth in published work.

The point of our detour is to illustrate that the popular idea that psychology and religion operate in totally opposed or separated worlds is not true. To be sure there is still a reluctance in some psychologists to engage in conversation with theology. But the fact of religious experience as a proper subject of interest to psychologists is not in doubt.

Of course, the way religious experiences are interpreted by psychologists varies greatly, depending on their ideological assumptions. Some, like Freud, see religion in terms of a psychological prop which the mature might grow out of. Others, like Jung, realize that a spiritual dimension to life is a major component in our humanness. One more recent approach, which sought more to describe than to interpret, is found in the work of what was initially called the Religious Experience Research Unit, established in 1969 at Manchester College, Oxford.

This Unit was founded by Alistair Hardy, formerly professor of zoology at Oxford, to study contemporary religious experiences of people who voluntarily responded to requests for self-reports. He asked for information on individuals' experiences of 'being aware of a presence or power that is different from the everyday self'. In 1979 he published *The Spiritual Nature of Man*, which classified several thousand responses, and indicated a widespread acknowledgement of a transcendent reality, of the power of prayer, and of positive feelings of security and well-being often associated with religious experience. In *Exploring Inner Space* (1982), David Hay took Hardy's methods further, outlining research conducted in Nottingham, concluding that 'even in a period when the tattered remains of an ancient interpretative system are all that is left to most people, it is clear that religious experience still appears with extraordinary frequency' (cf. also Hay, 1990). In fact, he gave evidence of much more widespread acknowledgement of religious experience than most people would expect. The Religious Experience Research Unit is now the Alistair Hardy Centre at Westminster College, Oxford. From the different discipline of sociology, Grace Davie recently reported some research on the religious life of people in contemporary Britain, and concluded that about 70 per cent of the British population still say that they believe in God. (This is of course in marked contrast to the much lower percentage of people who belong to any kind of institutional religious community. Grace Davie (1994) called it 'believing without belonging'.)

So what is religion?

Psychology of religion is not without its problems.

First, what is religion? What do psychologists of religion think they are investigating? As early as 1912, Leuba reported 48 different definitions of religion in the literature. Nearly every book on the psychology of religion offers its own. Daniel Batson and Larry Ventis, for example, in their book *The Religious Experience* (1982), offer a functional approach: religion is 'whatever we as individuals do to come to grips personally with the questions that confront us because we are aware that we and others like us are alive and that we will die'.

Is 'religion' to be broad enough to cover everything that seems to touch on the paranormal, mystical and unconscious, as well as the attitudes and behaviour patterns of ordinary down-to-earth Christian people? Does it cover atheistic ideologies which raise existential questions, or is it restricted to systems of thought and values which are explicitly related to the existence of God or a god? Are drug-induced experiences which enhance a person's claimed religious awareness, themselves authentically 'religious'? There are some thorny questions of definition.

Then, second, there is a problem of method. How is a scientist to collect data about religion? William James based his work on biographies and self-reports, and though he called it 'empirical' it lacks the quantification and control of more contemporary empirical scientific methods. Recent investigators have used questionnaires, pencil and paper tests and statistical analyses, but these are open to all the uncertainties of such methods, and, perhaps especially in religion, the probabilities of telling the questioner what you think they want to hear; in other words, of self-deceit and the desire for social approval. Various techniques have been devised to try to make the results more objective, but the methods are still not very sophisticated. Are we faced with a choice between a phenomenological approach, which allows religious people to disclose their experiences and then seeks to analyse and evaluate these phenomena (which can hardly be called 'scientific'), and an empirical scientific approach, which is limited to what can be observed and measured ('religiosity'), but in which the heart of religious experience escapes from view, leaving us, some would argue, with what is often merely trivial or boring? Batson and Ventis themselves try to overcome the problem by noting that the unobservable features of inner personal religious experience none the less leave observable tracks which are open to measurement. 'So long as religious experience in all its individuality, transcendence and mystery leaves observable tracks or symptoms, it is amenable to empirical analysis.'

Underlying these questions of definition and method, however, is a much deeper problem. Behind all psychologies and behind all psychological methods of investigation, there are certain assumptions about the nature of the object of investigation and of our basic interpretative framework, or world view. In other words there is a certain view of human nature implicit in the processes of psychological investigation, and many of the disagreements concerning definition and method arise from lack of agreement about the inner nature of the human subject which is the object of study. The fundamental issues of definition and method are not psychological or scientific, they are *theological*. The strong words of Orlo Strunk, himself a psychologist of religion, as long ago as 1980, still bear repeating:

> One of the major reasons for the severe paucity of inter-disciplinary research in the psychology of religion has been the tight conceptual framework of the psychologist of religion. Often controlled by a behaviouristic bias, frequently motivated by a reductionistic wish, and sometimes intoxicated by a crass positivism, he has found it impossible to communicate with those disciplines which move outside the constellation of such assumptions – especially theology proper. (Strunk, 1980)

He is criticizing those psychologists who start from the assumption that the experience of God may not be about God at all, but must, of course, be only a matter of our human make-up.

And yet it often escapes people's notice that one of the simplest explanations for the widespread religious experience of human beings is that it reflects in a rich variety of different ways the reality of the existence of God. Just as we may think it unhelpful to try to explain all biology in terms of physics and chemistry, so we may wonder why so many people try to explain experiences of God only in terms of psychological mechanisms, however important such mechanisms may be in those experiences.

William James was wiser here than some of his successors:

Medical materialism seems indeed a good appellation for the

too simple minded system of thought which we are considering. Medical materialism finishes up Saint Paul by calling
his vision on the road to Damascus a discharging lesion of
the occipital cortex, he being an epileptic. It snuffs out Saint
Teresa as an hysteric, Saint Francis of Assisi as an hereditary
degenerate. George Fox's discontent with the shams of his
age, and his pining for spiritual veracity, it treats as a symptom
of a disordered colon ... Modern psychology, finding definite
psycho-physical connections to hold good, assumes as a convenient hypothesis that the dependence of mental states upon
bodily conditions must be thoroughgoing and complete ... But
now, I ask you, how can such an existential account of facts of
mental history decide in one way or another upon their spiritual
significance? (James, 1952, p. 14)

What was important for James is that religious experience has
a human and a divine component, and that psychology as such
can only study the former. A more recent psychologist, R. W.
Hood (1991, pp. 99ff.), gives as one of his fundamental
convictions that religions exist because of the necessity ade-
quately to express people's inalienable mystical natures. Hood
means that religious claims to truth must be taken seriously
within the psychology of religion. It does not mean that one
can empirically test a religion. 'It does mean that if religions
are claims to truth and are to be taken seriously, critical theory
must incorporate theologically informed variables.' Hood
concludes by referring to John Bowker's comment in *The
Sense of God* that in the various scientific claims to the origin
of the sense of god, no investigator has really taken seriously
that the origin of the sense of god might be God!

'Put bluntly,' Hood writes, 'psychologists will have to take
the possibility of God more seriously as a truth claim if their
research is to be meaningful ... And that realm within which
attributions to and about God are taken seriously as claims to
truth is theology.'

The biophysicist Arthur Peacocke put it like this:

Man in his religious activity is the whole man interacting

fully as a person ('body, mind and soul') with other people, who are equally totally interacting with him. Together they interact with the natural world and discover its meaning for them – and express the ultimacy of the significance of this complex integrated activity in their worshipful recognition of a transcendent, yet immanent, Creator as the source of all that is. (Peacocke, 1979, p. 369)

Another glimpse of God

The fact of religious experience as part of human experience can function, it seems to me – to use the language which we used in the last chapter – as a glimpse of God. The fact that personal relationships are supremely important to us points to the fact that personal relationships are at the heart of things. The mystery of what goes on in a developing child's relationship with her parents, for example, points beyond to the mystery of why personal relationships are important at all.

The Dutch theologian Heije Faber (1976) emphasizes how much of psychoanalytic theory takes very seriously the importance of relationships in early life. What the Freudians call the Oedipus phase of development draws attention to the basic feelings, jealousies and angers that are around between father, child and mother in the early years of a child's life. Freud himself tried to explain the religious feelings of human beings by reference back to the importance of the 'infantile bond' and projected feelings about a Father-figure. Faber comments that Freud 'tries to explain one mystery by another'. Faber then goes on to turn this round. 'We would rather say that the sacred mystery already proclaims itself in the infantile bond and that, where development is normal, this develops into a mature relationship with God' (Faber, 1976, p. 241). In other words, the mystery of human interrelationships is so significant, precisely because they reflect something of the fact that the heart of the universe (God) is relational.

And here Christian faith, with its understanding of God as a Trinity of persons in relationship, gives us a top-down view of how things are.

In his Pelican book on psychology of personality, Peter Morea (1990) concludes with this statement:

> The mystery of personality points to a personal God ... in examining and analysing personality scientifically, we confront boundaries and encounter a mystery ... If human beings are made in God's image it would explain why we sometimes sense beyond the mystery of human personality a much greater Mystery: God himself.

Psychological science, I think, can serve as a signal of transcendence, can encourage us to interpret some of our experiences as a glimpse of God.

Perhaps Jonathan Edwards, philosopher, preacher, theologian, the 'founding father of the psychology of religion', inspiration for William James, should give us the last words:

> What is the nature of true religion? and wherein lie the distinguishing marks of that virtue which is acceptable in the sight of God? ...
>
> True religion, in great part, consists in holy affections ...
>
> God has given to mankind affections for the same purpose as that for which he has given all the faculties and principles of the human soul, viz., that they might be subservient to man's chief end, and the great business for which God has created him, that is, the business of religion.
>
> Affections that are truly spiritual and gracious arise from those influences and operations on the heart, which are spiritual, supernatural and divine ...
>
> It is doubtless true and evident from the Scriptures that the essence of all true religion lies in holy love; and that in this divine affection – and habitual disposition to it, that light which is the foundation to it, and those things which are its fruits – consists the whole of religion. (Edwards, 1746)

And if that is the case, then part of the mission of the Church will be to seek to provide a context in which 'religious affections' can develop and grow – how in other words people can be enabled to become (in Irenaeus' terms) more fully alive.

Chapter 3
GOD SO LOVED THE WORLD

We are attempting to explore something of the reason-ableness of Christian faith and something of the nature of Christian mission in the contemporary world by rather loosely using the themes of John 3.16 as pegs on which to hang our discussion. We have indicated some of the ways in which our human experience may give us glimpses of the God who is most clearly made known in Jesus Christ. We have suggested that religious experience can often itself best be understood in terms of the reality of God. It is now time to move on through the themes of our text, and look at some aspects of the world which God loves.

If we were able to ask the author of John's Gospel what he means by 'the world' we would probably get several different answers. Sometimes John means 'human nature organized without reference to God'. This is the world which, along with the flesh and the devil, we are often exhorted to resist. In Iris Murdoch's novel *The Green Knight* Bellamy has given away his dog to Louise, because 'he had decided in the middle of life's journey to abandon the world and become some sort of religious person'.

To 'abandon the world and become some sort of religious person'. This is how some Christian people use the word 'world', as something to be abandoned. This is certainly one strand of Christian attitudes to the world. Some Christian communities have taken the biblical injunction to 'come apart and be separate' as a political programme for an alternative society. Some of the teaching of Menno Simmons, founder of the Mennonites; some of the lifestyle of groups such as the Amish in Indiana, suggest that a Christian response to 'the world' should be an avertive one of withdrawal and distinction.

49

A second theme in the Fourth Gospel is that the world is seen as an arena for mission. In chapter 17, Jesus prays: 'As thou didst send me into the world, so I have sent them into the world … I pray … that they may all be one; … so that the world may believe.' This emphasis is the opposite of 'avertive' – it is rather that Christian engagement with the world should be 'transformative'. It is a 'transformative' view of the world for which I wish to argue in this chapter. However, we need to be careful, since some Christian modes of mission have not been without their problems. Take another picture, this time from Dickens's *Bleak House*, in which Mrs Jellyby is described as 'a lady of very remarkable strength of character who devotes herself entirely to the public. She is at present devoted to the subject of Africa; with a view to the general cultivation of the coffee berry – and the natives – and the happy settlement on the banks of the African rivers, of our superabundant home population.' Mrs Jellyby is described as a lady of 'rapacious benevolence' – another attitude to the world – one which is perhaps seen most in the complicated links between nineteenth-century missionary movements and the growth of British imperialism. 'The world' was somewhere to be done good to, and, of our benevolence, we sought to do it.

But there is a third, important, use of 'the world' in the Fourth Gospel. In John chapter 1 we read: 'He was in the world, and the world was made through him' – the world in other words is the whole created order. More specifically, it means the world of human beings: 'This is indeed the prophet who is to come into the world!' And it is this sense in which John 3.16 gives us: 'God so loved the world', and in 4.42: 'we know that this is indeed the Saviour of the world'.

This is a transformative approach to the world, but one which respects the world as the sphere of God's creative and redemptive love, and seeks in our human response to the world to reflect something of God's love for it.

When we read that God so loved the world, we do not, like Bellamy, mean something to be rejected, nor only, like Mrs Jellyby, something to be ministered to. We mean the whole created order which God loves, the world in which Christ's light shines, and of which we can affirm him Saviour. It is also the world from which we can and must learn: – for 'The true light that enlightens everyone was coming into the world' (John 1.9). Throughout the whole created order God's light shines, and just as we are invited to be caught up into sharing what we know of that light with others, so we must be open to receiving that light from other parts of God's world.

The mission of the Church of Jesus Christ is a mission from the Father in the name of the Son and in the power of the Spirit for the sake of the world. The Kingdom, we noted, is creation healed. The mission of the Church will therefore need to engage with the difficulties many people in contemporary culture have in making any link at all between God and the world, not least through the popular belief that science has made belief in God impossible. The first part of this chapter will therefore look at some of the supposed difficulties which the world of science poses for Christian faith. We will then select one other area in which if God so loved the world, Christian people, it seems to me, must take a very special interest, namely world poverty.

The world of science

There is a significant hurdle to be jumped for many people in our culture in making any link at all between God and the world. The hurdle is the supposed barrier created by the development and apparent success of science. Has not science shown that belief in the creator is impossible? Do not articulate contemporary scientists such as Richard Dawkins in *The Selfish Gene* (1978) and *The Blind Watchmaker* (1991), and Peter Atkins in *Creation Revisited* (1994), pour scorn – in the name of science – on those who hold to a religious view of the world? In so far as they do, thankfully they are not representative of the whole scientific community, among whom many are Christian believers, and for whom the work of science is their response to the creativity of God.

About ten years ago, the Society of Ordained Scientists was formed. It is now made up of about 70 research scientists, physicists, chemists, medical physiologists, geologists, biologists and so on, who are ordained priests or deacons in the Church of England, and in one or two other denominations. One was the head of a Cambridge College – a former professor of mathematical physics who was ordained, one was an archbishop who used to be a research scientist at Cambridge, two were on the staff of cathedrals, one was a research chemist for Guinness the brewers, some were hospital chaplains, one was a consultant for NASA, the American space agency in Texas, one was a schoolteacher, in charge of chemistry and religious studies at a major public school, one was a pathologist, one a lecturer in genetics, and so on. All are ordained in the Church's ministry; all have research degrees in science. The Society meets each year for a retreat to talk and pray; its aims are:

> To offer to God in our ordained role the work of science in the exploration and stewardship of creation; to express the commitment of the church to the scientific enterprise and our concern for its impact on the world, to develop a fellowship of prayer for ordained scientists, to support each other in our vocation; to serve the church in its relation to science and technology.

The existence of this Society is itself a signal that faith and science need not be enemies.

It is worth exploring three aspects of the relationship between science and religion: history, cosmology and belief.

History

First, some thoughts on history: why did what we now call modern science come to birth when and where it did in seventeenth-century Europe?[1]

There were the beginnings of science in ancient Greece, Rome, Persia, China; certainly mathematics in the Arab world. But it did not last. Any science was still-born. In the ancient world we find impressive art and architecture, highly developed technical skills, metal work, ceramics, stone. There is skill in land measurement, knowledge of the stars. But none of this became what we call science – a way of understanding nature through exploration, through forming hypotheses and making predictions, and expressing the knowledge we gain quantitatively in mathematics.

So we must ask the question, why did science come to birth and grow where and when it did in seventeenth-century Europe and not in the ancient world? The detailed understanding of nature that we call science first developed and came to maturity at a very definite point in human history. It was primarily the achievement of Newton, who built on the work of Copernicus, Kepler and Galileo. He formulated laws of motion and showed how these could be used to calculate the fall of an apple and the orbit of the moon. He also developed the mathematical technique called differential calculus, and used this to express his laws of motion in a concise and elegant form. He laid the foundations of theoretical physics, and the extraordinary growth of science since his time has been essentially a development of the experimental methods used by him.

So what is needed for science to develop? What conditions, asks Peter Hodgson, a nuclear physicist, are necessary to prevent science being still-born? He replies: You need a well enough developed society so that people have time to think about things, and not just worry about staying alive. You need to be able to make experiments so you need a good enough technology to construct apparatus. You need to have sufficient mathematics and be able to record your results in a convenient way. You need to have good enough communication between different workers in the community of science for your results to be checked and agreed. These are what we might call the 'material conditions' needed for science. But these can be found in the ancient world, in earlier civilizations.

What was it that made seventeenth-century Europe different? It was in the realm of ideas. A number of writers have suggested that it was the ideas that were around at that time in

Europe that made science possible. And most of those key ideas came from Christian faith.

If you felt the material world was evil, as some of the Greeks did, you would not have incentive to explore it. If you believed there was no order in the world, science would not be possible. If you believed that everything was just one fatalistic cycle after another, as some Eastern philosophies did, nothing actually matters, and there would be no incentive for doing something as decisive as setting up an experiment, there would be no curiosity to explore. But Christian faith, shared by many of the first members of the Royal Society – who, to use Kepler's phrase, said they were 'thinking God's thoughts after him' – contributed to a set of ideas which were conducive to the growth and viability of experimental science.

For example:

- The Christian view of the world, as described in the lovely creation poem in Genesis 1, depicts a beautifully ordered world of which God says 'This is good.' If God says the world is good, then let us get out and explore God's creation.
- The Christian view of history, with a beginning and a middle and an end: history has a direction. Christianity says this is not an eternally oscillating universe, nor a fatalistic cycle in which nothing matters. In the Christian linear view of history everything matters. That gives the scientist an incentive, a purpose, a motivation to act.
- The Christian view of grace: if God turns towards his world in grace, should we not turn towards it in gratitude?
- The Christian view of rationality. Is it not an extraordinary thing that science works at all? How can it be that our minds can find the world intelligible? Einstein once said, with some degree of poetic licence, 'The only incomprehensible thing about the universe is that it is comprehensible.' Arthur Peacocke, whom I mentioned, asks 'Why should science work at all? That it does so points strongly to a principle of rationality, to an interpretation of the cosmos in terms of mind as its most significant feature' (Peacocke, 1971, pp. 133f.). A Christian theology can begin to make sense of this

by recognizing that the rational order of the world out there, and the rational order of our minds, both derive from the creative rationality of God, expressing what John's Gospel calls 'Logos' – the Word.

None of this, of course, proves that Christian faith caused the development of science. That would be much too strong a claim. But it does say that in the realm of ideas in sixteenth- and seventeenth-century Europe, when science was born, there was tremendous encouragement from Christian faith for science, which enabled it to be viable and not – as in some other civilizations – die at birth.

This is what Robert Boyle, of the famous Boyle's Law, said in 1685: 'There are two chief ways to arrive at knowledge of God's attributes; the contemplation of his works, and the study of his word' (quoted in Peacocke, 1979, p. 4). And the biologist John Ray in 1691 wrote a book called *The Wisdom of God Manifested in the Works of Creation* (Peacocke, 1979, p. 4).

So has science disproved religion? Many of the great founders of modern science would put it quite the other way round: it is Christian faith that has enabled science to grow.

Cosmology
Second, we move to cosmology, and reflect on some more recent work on the origin of the universe.

Most cosmologists reckon that our universe started about 15,000 million years ago. It was an expanding ball of energy derived from what is often called the Big Bang. Some have suggested that its ending will be a reversal of that expansion, with the universe collapsing back into itself – the Big Crunch. Happily that is also a few thousand million years away. But the remarkable thing is that the universe we experience now is a rich, varied, complicated place, and one of the most remark- able and complicated things about it is that you and I are here. In some of his writings John Polkinghorne (e.g. 1986; 1988; 1989; 1991; 1994) tries a little thought experiment. He wonders what would have happened if the force of gravity had been stronger than it is. Or what would have happened if electro-

magnetism was a bit weaker. The answer is that the expansion
rate of the universe, and the chemicals that constitute it, would
have been very different. If there had been very small changes
in various of what are called universal constants (gravity,
electromagnetism, velocity of light, nuclear forces and so on –
features of the make-up of our universe), we would not be here.
For people like us, who can think and make relationships and
fall in love, and hold discussions about science, in other words
for carbon-based organic life, which is what we are, to come
into being, you would need the nuclear furnaces which we call
the stars to burn for a very long time. These furnaces develop
the heavier elements like carbon and oxygen from the very
simple ones like hydrogen and helium; and it can be calculated
that it takes several thousand million years for the nuclear and
chemical processes needed to bring carbon-based life into
being. Polkinghorne argues that while we do not live at the
centre of the universe, neither do we live in just any old world.
We live in a universe whose constitution is precisely adjusted to
the narrow limits which alone would make it capable of being
our home (cf. Polkinghorne, 1988, pp. 22ff.).

Or let me quote also from Sir Bernard Lovell, former
director of Jodrell Bank:

> Why is the universe expanding so near the critical rate to
> prevent its collapse? If the universe had begun to expand in
> the first few minutes after the explosion of its originally
> incredibly dense state by a rate minutely slower than it
> did, it would have collapsed back again relatively quickly.
> And if the expansion of the universe had been different only
> by a tiny fraction one way or the other from its actual rate,
> human existence would evidently have been impossible. But
> our measurements narrowly define one such universe, which
> had to be that particular universe if it was ever to be known
> and comprehended by an intelligent being. (Lovell, 1977,
> quoted by Torrance, 1980, p. 3)

This is what some people call 'the anthropic principle'[2]: the
idea that the way the universe is is somehow tied up with the

emergence of human life. We and the universe are profoundly bracketed together. In fact, science itself seems to be pointing to the importance of personal life.

Now once again, we cannot move from this to say, 'That proves God exists.' What we can do is say, 'The Christian view of this universe, that it derives and is held in being by a God who is personal, who in the Holy Trinity is described as persons in relationships of love, this view fits in very well with the picture that is emerging from the cosmology of the anthropic principle.'

One other remarkable development in recent years has been what is somewhat unhelpfully called 'chaos theory'. In briefest, and oversimplified outline, we can approach the issue like this: Isaac Newton's view of the cosmos was of a large machine which worked according to predictable laws. God wound up the clockwork and left it to tick. From the work of Einstein and others at the start of the twentieth century, it became clear that the clockwork universe, the world as a super machine as Newton had envisaged, had to be replaced by a view of the world which at the atomic level is uncertain and unpredictable. We cannot tell both the velocity and the position of any particular electron. More recently still, scientists have realized this unpredictability applies also to the world of everyday experience. Many of the things we thought worked according to predictable physical laws are actually not predictable.

One of the starting points for this was study of the weather. It is sometimes called the butterfly effect. The weather systems turn out to be so sensitive that a butterfly stirring the air with its wings in China today will affect the weather storms over England in a few weeks' time. Since we cannot possibly know about all the Chinese butterflies, we cannot reliably predict what will happen in the future. That is why it is called 'chaos' (e.g. Gleick, 1987). It is a combination of certain physical laws, and a profound uncertainty of other things: Chance and Necessity working together. And yet the chaos itself throws up new and unpredictable demonstrations of order – illustrated perhaps by the way several hundred ants running in apparently haphazard fashion can none the less produce the unpredictable order of an ants' nest. There is an order to our weather systems, but one that is not wholly predictable.

In a very real sense the future is open; the world that science is opening up is much more dynamic, fruitful, open and interconnected than the mechanical world of Newton. In other words, science is pointing us beyond traditional analytical science – to see things not only in terms of the parts which we can analyse, but in terms of the wholes of things in their interrelationships and interconnectedness.

And this, of course, is exciting for a Christian, because to believe in God means that relationships are all important – between me and my environment, me and my neighbour, me and God. The physical, emotional, moral and spiritual dimensions to life are all important. And that moves me on to a further set of ideas. And the wholistic dimensions of recent theories of chaos and complexity (e.g. Waldrop, 1992) give a language within which an understanding of interrelationships can be expressed.

Christian faith believes that there are many different levels to our understanding of the world, and all are important, and all belong together. The Word was made flesh right down to the level of our genes. One example might illustrate the point: my wedding ring. There are many dimensions of understanding what my wedding ring is.

- At one level, the spatial dimensions: this is a circle about 2 cm across;
- at the physical level: this has a certain weight and density;
- at the chemical level: this is gold.

But there is more to this ring than this.

- It has a history. Presumably it was dug up out of the ground as a lump of gold and was refined and shaped and moulded and found its way to a jeweller's shop in Vale Road, Tunbridge Wells.
- It has an emotional significance. It was given to me by a

special person on a special day when certain promises were made.

- It has a social significance. It tells any other prospective admirers that I am already committed.
- It has a spiritual purpose: reminding me of the endlessness of God's covenant love, and calling me to remain faithful in my love.

There are many levels: all important. The key point is that the higher levels are dependent on, but not reducible to, the lower ones. Only some of them are appropriately called scientific in the usual sense. By and large science tends to try to analyse things down to the lowest level of explanation. But it will not do to say 'this is nothing but a lump of gold', any more than it will do to say that Yehudi Menuhin playing the Mendelssohn Violin Concerto is doing 'nothing more' than scraping the hairs of one animal over the gut of another; any more than it will do to say that persons in relationships of love are nothing more than physics and chemistry. In Sartre's *Age of Reason*, Boris has just 'made love' to Lola. Then he says, 'It's just physiology; just physiology.' The reader is left with a sense of sadness that that is all. The reader knows that personal love is more than physiology. Reductionism will not do.

This is a major point of dispute between Christian thinkers, and scientists such as Richard Dawkins and Peter Atkins. As Keith Ward (1996) has demonstrated convincingly, both Dawkins's *Blind Watchmaker* and Atkins's *Creation Revisited*, brilliant though they are in some respects, are logically flawed at a number of points, not least in relation to the reductionist fallacy.

Perhaps science tends to work from the bottom up; perhaps theology tends to work from the top down. Another commonly used illustration makes the point: a boiling kettle in the kitchen.

Why is that kettle boiling? Because the heat from the gas is affecting the vapour pressure in the water and the water is undergoing a change of state.

Why is that kettle boiling? Because I am making a cup of tea.

Both answers are true at their own level. But the top-down view also includes the note of purpose. A Christian picture of the world has a place for the scientific levels of understanding, but wants to see them as part of a bigger picture, a picture which includes God's purpose as part of the whole story.

The nature of belief

The third dimension to this discussion concerns the nature of belief. I want to suggest that science itself is based on commitment and faith.

Some people say that the world of science is the world of sure and certain agreed facts; the world of religion is one of private untestable beliefs. Science, people say, works by tidy predictable processes of experiment, hypothesis, testing, verification. Most research scientists may hold to this as an ideal, but know that the processes of discovery are much less straightforward. In practice, science is often about getting it wrong and trying again, about having an idea in the bath, about a hunch that you need to try out, about results that don't fit in with your theory and having to think again. Occasionally when things work, there is a tremendous sense of excitement and thrill. More usually there can be frustration and hard work.

In other words, scientific knowledge, like all knowlege, has an inescapably personal aspect to it. The personal involvement of the scientist in the process of knowing is inevitable.[3] The scientist tries very hard to be as objective as possible, so that if his experiment is repeated by other people in other places under relevantly similar conditions they should get the same results. But there are always the personal judgements that are made, the personal skills that are developed, the intuition and the insights which guide research. And those are not scientific categories. They are personal categories. And underneath these personal dimensions to knowing there are certain commitments. The scientist operates with a framework of beliefs to which she commits herself. There are fundamental assumptions on which science is built – for example, that the world is *ordered* and *contingent*.

By an *ordered* world, I mean that there are discoverable patterns which make some prediction possible. Even in what I was earlier saying about chaos, there is the possibility of the emergence of a different sort of order. Out of chance and necessity emerge wonderfully unexpected things, a richer sort of order: the order of things as wholes, not just as parts. No one can predict the exact pattern of a single snowflake; all are different. But there is a wonderful order underlying the variety. No one can predict which way any one ant will run around the ants' nest, but there is an order to the nest as a whole. There is in fact a more profound, more complicated, even if more uncertain, order to the world than earlier scientists assumed. But science works on the assumptions that there is that about the world which makes sense. The writer of Genesis 1 gives us a picture of an ordered world which I think tells us that his way of thinking is not very far from the mind of science.

By a *contingent* world, I mean that it does not have to be the way it is. This means that one cannot discover anything about the world by sitting in a Greek philosopher's armchair and just thinking about it. If the order of the world were a necessary order, if it could not have been anything else, we might have discovered it by thinking. But because it is contingent, because it did not have to be this way, we have to explore it, do experiments on it, persuade nature to yield up its secrets. We have to discover what is there. The creation story also tells us that everything comes from God's word: He said, and it was so. In other words, the Bible opens up to us a contingent world: the order of this world does not have to be the way it is; it might have been different. A Christian will say it is the way it is because of God's choosing. And that is another motivation for our voyage of discovery.

But these assumptions, and others, are not scientific in themselves. We make a commitment to the belief that the world displays a certain order and will disclose itself to our exploration. These are basic beliefs without which science could not happen. Science, in other words, is 'faith seeking understanding' – to use a medieval phrase used to describe theology.

The two disciplines, theology and science, are not too far apart at this point. Both science and theology begin with commitments of faith. Both science and theology believe there is something beyond ourselves which will reveal itself to us. Both science and theology are attempts at understanding. Both are ways of exploring God's world; both belong together as allies not as enemies.

There are a significant number of scientists who see science itself as a signal of transcendence, pointing beyond the discoveries about the physical world to God the creator and source of all that is.

So has science disproved religion? I don't think so. The world out there and my inner world make more sense to me in the context of a much bigger, richer, more personal picture than science itself can offer, though to some degree science points towards it.

If, as I have argued, the mission of the Church of Jesus Christ is to be caught up into the foundational fact that God so loved the world, an engagement between the Christian faith and the world of science will be an essential part of our task. Through our scientific discoveries, and through laying bare the hidden order of the physical world, science itself can give a voice to all created things. We can use our science, as Professor Thomas Torrance once put it, 'to bring their mute rationalities into such articulation that the praises of the Creator may resound throughout the whole universe' (Torrance, 1971, p. 164).

It is not inappropriate to record the Collect of the Society of Ordained Scientists:

Almighty God, Creator and Redeemer of all that is, source and foundation of time and space, matter and energy, life and consciousness; Grant us in this Society, and all who study the mysteries of your creation, grace to be true witnesses to your glory and faithful stewards of your gifts; through Jesus Christ our Lord.

The world of poverty

If God so loved the world, part of our Christian mission is to engage with the real world, and alongside the programmes of scientific discovery, that also includes an engagement with the future of the planet and of human life upon it. This immediately, as we will note more fully in a moment, involves an acknowledgement that the uses of science in technology, industry and commerce have sometimes had a very destructive effect on the well-being of this planet. Ecological devastation and environmental pollution are the evil by-products of a failure to use science responsibly. The Tower of Babel (Genesis 11.1–9; cf. Atkinson, 1990) is sufficient to demonstrate the social damage that results from human beings trying to play at being God, and ending up simply building power structures of our own.

A major result of human sin and selfishness in the misuse of science and technology is world poverty. In 1996, over 30 of the leading voluntary and campaigning organizations in the UK, including Christian Aid, Oxfam, the Catholic Institute for International Relations, Church Action on Poverty, Quaker Social Responsibility and Education, World Wide Fund for Nature, United Nations Association (UK), and Save the Children Fund, produced a 'statement of public concern' called *The Politics of the Real World* (Real World Coalition, 1996). We will summarize their argument as the basis for this discussion.

There is a widespread mood of fear and anxiety about the future. These authors propose a political programme for sustainable development, social justice and democratic renewal. One of their major concerns is to show that the widespread assumption that the model of economic progress and growth on which Western governments base many of their policies is simply false. It has been thought that the principal purpose of economic activity is to raise incomes and create more consumption, and that through taxation, governments can then provide essential public services such as education and health care, and ultimately everyone benefits. But, they argue, this system is cracking.[4] Although some people become richer, others actually become poorer. And the effect world-wide of a commitment in the West to the motor of free trade is devastating.

> When 35,000 of the world's children die each day from preventable hunger and disease; when increasing inequality in Britain is leaving large numbers of the poor and un-employed permanently excluded from mainstream society; when human degradation of the environment is destroying the livelihoods and health of hundreds of millions of people in rich and poor countries, urban and rural areas alike – and when all these costs are getting larger, not smaller; then the morality of the cost–benefit calculus has reached its limit. (Real World Coalition, 1996, p. 11)

Furthermore, this is not only a matter of justice – it is also, the authors argue, a matter of self-interest: 'For the costs of the dominant model of global economic development are now beginning to outweigh its benefits, even for its beneficiaries' (Real World Coalition, 1996, p.11).

The current pattern of resource use and waste generation in industrialized societies is not sustainable. Most of the most serious environmental problems we face are not the result of technical failures in basically sound activities, but flow from the essential character of current production and consumption patterns. This requires governments to take with utmost seriousness

> the concept of 'sustainable' environmental limits; the need to integrate environmental and economic policy; the require-ment to take explicit political account of the future and to adapt government institutions to new conditions of complex-ity and uncertainty; the link between environmental degradation and poverty ... (Real World Coalition, 1996, p. 25)

Issues such as population control, world energy needs and

resources, the globalization of the economy, the unequal sharing of the benefits of 'development', are all interlinked.

After three decades of 'development', the facts of global poverty represent a shocking measure of failure. 1.3 billion people, more than a fifth of the human race, live in absolute poverty, lacking access to basic necessities such as food and clean drinking water. One third of the world's children are undernourished, and 12.2 million die before the age of five every year, 95 percent of them from poverty-related illnesses.

It cannot any longer be argued that pursuit of development based on economic growth will eliminate poverty – on the contrary, it seems to be increasing it. And increasing poverty generates new fields of conflict and tension, creating larger numbers of refugees and migrants. The international regime of free trade, capital mobility and market deregulation acts as a constant pressure on social and environmental standards. We need reform in the areas of aid, of international debt, of the philosophy underlying the regulation of international trade – particularly the arms trade – and international finance systems. The Politics of the Real World Coalition makes a strong plea for new domestic objectives in economic and political life which start with achieving environmental sustainability, reducing inequality and poverty, and increasing and redistributing employment and work. We are part of an interdependent world, and all of us are involved.

If the Christian Church is to share in the proclamation that God so loved the world we cannot avoid engaging with such global economic and environmental questions. Some writers have argued that it is the Christian faith itself which is responsible for much of the ecological crisis, with an interpretation of the Genesis mandate which apparently gives humanity 'dominion' over the rest of creation. It is true that some people have shamefully taken this to mean a licence to exploit the rest of the created order to serve human needs. The American historian Lyn White Jr has been widely quoted as describing Christianity as 'the most anthropocentric religion the world has seen' and as blaming the medieval Church for the current pollution of the environment. But others have pointed out that it was the commercial incentives arising from the Industrial Revolution which must bear the brunt of the blame. Most commentators on Genesis have made clear that the 'creation mandate' is for responsible stewardship of the rich resources of God's earth. To be made 'in the divine image' includes the responsibility for being God's 'estate manager' for the well-being of all creatures.

Christian mission in the light of God's love for the world, therefore, will take the ecological needs of the planet with utmost seriousness.[5] The additional clause at the end of the 1988 Lambeth Conference Report included these words: 'the mission of the church is to safeguard the integrity of creation and sustain and renew the life of the earth'.

This all throws into very sharp relief the growing and apparently insurmountable problems of international debt, and the call that was made to see the year 2000 as a Jubilee in which much Third World debt is cancelled.

Jubilee

In his very first encyclical published in 1979, Pope John Paul II referred to the year 2000 as a Great Jubilee. He has since said the same in his Apostolic Letter about the Millennium (John Paul II, 1994, para. 51). This is a theme which has been taken up by many different Christian groups.

One of the special events which marked community time in the Old Testament was the jubilee year (Leviticus 25.1–28). Every fifty years, so the law said, the fields were to lie fallow, property was to be returned to its original owners and slaves to be liberated. The theological rationale was that the land whose only lord was the Lord was given to his people that they might live together in freedom and community. The Jubilee regulation, whether or not it was ever enacted exactly in the form described in the Old Testament, was concerned with countering the tendency for land to accumulate in the hands only of a few. It was concerned with economic support for the household unit. It was concerned with providing a safety valve to release the pressure of economic forces on the poor (cf. Wright, 1990, pp. 123ff.; Logan, 1997). Jubilee was about liberty and restoration. The whole earth is given by God to humanity for responsible stewardship. The economy needs to support social justice in God's world.[6]

Jubilee underlies the Nazareth Manifesto of Jesus' mission of redemption: 'to preach good news to the poor ... to proclaim release to the captives and recovery of sight to the blind, to set at liberty those who are oppressed, to proclaim the acceptable year of the Lord' (Luke 4.18–19). I think it also underlies the way the fellowship of the New Testament Church was called to ensure an equitable distribution of resources 'that there may be equality', as St Paul puts it (2 Corinthians 8.9, 14). Jubilee theology requires us to think carefully about the needs of the poorest people, the environment, the disadvantaged, the homeless, those in debt, and to find a way of working towards a more just social structure and more just society.

The Pope himself proposed in his Apostolic Letter that the whole world should work for 'reducing substantially, if not cancelling outright, the international debt which seriously threatens the future of many nations'.

Perhaps a key theme in our thinking, to take us back again to the Old Testament Jubilee, is that of renewal. Christians can be renewed in solidarity with the poor. The new information technologies could be put to use precisely in developing new networks for social justice, environmental action and campaigns on behalf of the powerless and the marginalized. Christian mission must be seeking to discern what God is asking of us – in penitence for past mistakes, and in promoting debate about the sort of world of which God wishes us to be stewards in the future.

This world, then, is something to be loved with the love of God, something to be prayed for, engaged with and learned from. This means an open-hearted commitment to the stewardship responsibilities of being made in God's image. It means an openness to the divine light and word wherever that is manifested in the created order. It means a willingness to set aside the sort of worldliness which tries to organize human society without reference to God. It means a commitment to the sort of love for our neighbour which shows itself in a passion for justice in all human affairs – the love through which the world comes to see something of God. It means bearing our witness to the one whom John describes as 'the Saviour of the world'. And it means not withdrawal but engagement. As the seventeenth-century poet Thomas Traherne (1908) put it:

> By an act of understanding therefore be present now with all the creatures among which you live; and hear them in their beings and operations praising God. Some of them vocally, others in their ministry, all of them naturally and continually.
>
> We infinitely wrong ourselves by laziness and confinement.
>
> All creatures in all nations and tongues and people praise God infinitely ... You are never what you ought till you go out of yourself and walk among them.

God so loved the world.

Chapter 4

GOD SO LOVED … THAT HE GAVE

The heart of Christian faith, Christian life and Christian mission is the love of God.

It is to an exploration of love – and particularly the objectivity of love in action in the world – that we now turn our attention, having in mind that the 'modern' world finds it hard to see moral value as anything other than private and personal. If Christian faith is to speak of a God who so loved that he gave, we are going to find ourselves in dialogue with those for whom morality is a question only of relative truths and subjective decisions.

'Love' is one of those portmanteau words which carry a very wide range of meanings. It can express sheer sentimentality – often traded on by the advertisers ('All because the lady loves Milk Tray'). It is sometimes used just to express delight or pleasure ('I love that dress'). It can be a word which overlaps with erotic feelings ('make love'), or which expresses family affection and commitment ('Lots of love, Mummy'). In Christian literature all these are found, but there is a distinctive way in which New Testament writers use the Greek word *agape*, the word usually used to describe the love of God. *Agape* is best understood, almost defined, by a text in the First Letter of John: 'In this is love, not that we loved God but that he loved us and sent his Son to be the expiation for our sins. Beloved, if God so loved us, we also ought to love one another' (1 John 4.10–11). The heart of the New Testament meaning of *agape* is that the love which God shows for the world, and for us, and which to some degree includes and transforms all the other forms of love, is that the love of God is self-giving. Whereas *eros* often depends on and responds to some value (beauty, worth), seen in the object which is loved, and is often focused on the lover, *agape* is usually more related to sacrificial giving, irrespective of whether the object deserves the love that is given. Sometimes even through the act of loving, *agape* creates value in that object. George Herbert's poem 'Love III' illustrates this:

Love bade me welcome: yet my soul drew back,
　　Guilty of dust and sin.
But quick-ey'd Love, observing me grow slack
　　From my first entrance in,
Drew nearer to me, sweetly questioning,
　　If I lack'd anything.

A guest, I answer'd, worthy to be here:
　　Love said, You shall be he.
I the unkind, ungrateful? Ah my dear,
　　I cannot look on thee.
Love took my hand, and smiling did reply,
　　Who made the eyes but I?

Truth Lord, but I have marr'd them: let my shame
　　Go where it doth deserve.
And know you not, says Love, who bore the blame?
　　My dear, then I will serve.
You must sit down, says Love, and taste my meat:
　　So I did sit and eat.

We may say that *agape* is disinterested, though not in the sense that *agape* does not care. *Agape* is disinterested in the sense that there is no self-interest in the one who shows love. We see this in the life and ministry of Jesus. His warm-hearted compassion affects all he says and does in relation to people whom he seeks to reach with the love of God. He is depicted in the Gospels as having compassion on the crowds, and ministering to the sick, as eating with outcasts, as breaking through taboos to touch lepers, as grieving at a family grave, as loving his friends to the uttermost. Greater love has no man than this, that a man lay down his life for his friends.

Agape, then, according to the Gospel, is demonstrated love –

given to the world and to us by God, irrespective of whether we deserve it, notice it, want it or receive it. God's self-giving love does not depend on our feelings. In that sense it is 'objective' – it is there, given, whether we like it or not.

As an illustration, notice how the word 'given' is used in the Church Marriage Service – 'marriage is given that ...'. It assumes an objectively given moral order within which the couple now make their vows. This is the sense in which we are talking of the 'objective', 'given' love of God.

To talk about 'objective' love – indeed to talk about any 'objective' moral value – is to go against the grain of much modern and post-modern thinking. Here is another Christian assumption which has been widely challenged in our con-temporary cultures. We will do well to stand back from this for a while, and consider what we mean by 'objectivity' in relation to moral values – for here, it seems to me, is another significant pointer in our human experience, which points beyond itself to the reality of God, but one which much of our contemporary culture has forgotten, or refuses to see.

First, a few words about what we mean by 'morality'. 'Morality' is a word which describes not only how people behave, but how we think they ought to behave. There is a sense of obligation. We are dealing with such words as 'right' and 'wrong', 'good' and 'bad' and 'duty'. And we could be talking about attitudes (I don't like Jim), motives (I want to get back at Jim for what he did to me), intentions (I will hurt him), actions (I hit him over the head with a cricket bat) or consequences (Jim has a bruised head, the police have my description, I have a guilty conscience). In fact in most moral situations, all of these dimensions are present.

The question I want to focus on here is where we get our sense of right and wrong from. For some people, this has come from 'nature' (evolutionary ethics); for others, from 'society'; for long centuries of Christian tradition, the moral sense has been understood to come from God – either through the moral law which he implants in our consciences, or through the word of Scripture which educates our minds and wills, or through the inner witness of the Holy Spirit. In all these, and others, the source of moral values comes from outside us – it is 'given' to us, we receive it and decide whether or not to respond to it.

But the coming of 'modernity' changed all that. There was a significant move towards seeing morality not as something related 'objectively' to God, but as something which we create for ourselves.

As I write there is a debate in Parliament concerning fox-hunting. Some people are wanting fox-hunting made a criminal offence because it is a cruel and inhumane sport and human beings should not be allowed to gain pleasure by inflicting cruelty on other living creatures. Some people are wanting to maintain the cultural heritage of fox-hunting as a valued pastime which also helps maintain the rural ecology by keeping down the number of predators which threaten other livestock. There is, though, an interesting letter in today's paper which argues that because 'the general public' is not damaged by hunting it is none of anybody's business to intervene in what other people decide to do.

> Opinion polls show that a majority of the general public disapproves of a great many things, including the Conservative Party, homosexual acts, black pudding, smoking, immigration, Radio 3 and, very likely, the colour of my front door. If all these, and more, are to be made criminal because a majority does not like them, we shall all be in jail before long.

This letter seems to suggest that the writer believes (wrongly in my view) that moral questions only arise if people are damaged by something, and also (rightly) that moral questions cannot be decided by majority vote. He believes that if questions are to be decided by majority vote it means that questions concerning the colour of someone's skin become no more and no less important than the question of the colour of someone's front door. It seems as though the writer is – perhaps unwittingly – pointing to the fact that we need other grounds than simply personal taste, or majority preference, on which to handle moral questions.

And yet many people do at least pay lip service to the 'modern' view that morality is simply a matter of personal preference and taste. There was a book published some years ago with the title *Ethics: Inventing Right and Wrong*.[1] Are moral values something we invent, or something which is given?

Morality – a signal of transcendence

When we are confronted by something we must name as evil, we know that we are doing more than simply saying we do not like that sort of thing. You may like coffee; I prefer tea, and we can agree to differ about that. That is simply a matter of personal preferences. But when we are faced with a gunman shooting at random into a classroom of innocent schoolchildren, we want to say more than we 'don't like that sort of thing'. There is something objectively and ultimately wrong. Ethnic cleansing in Bosnia or Kosovo is not something which offends against good taste, and which most of us don't like: it is evil. And when I name it as evil, I am not simply expressing how I feel, I am saying something about the world outside myself which confronts me with an objectively evil fact.

To turn this round the other way: when I praise Princess Diana for her work in bringing the horrors of landmines to international attention; when I honour Mother Teresa for her self-sacrificing life in the back-streets of Calcutta, when I am faced with Dietrich Bonhoeffer's brave stand against the Nazi tyranny in a way which cost him his life, when I read of Jesus touching the lepers and having compassion on the crowds, and I call this 'good' – I am saying something about Princess Diana and Mother Teresa and Bonhoeffer and Jesus – I am doing more than saying I happen to like what they did. There is some objective goodness which confronts me and before which I am obliged to make a response (cf. Owen, 1965).

The difficulty of the modern world which seeks to make morality a subjective matter, and in which I invent right and wrong (and even more of the post-modern world in which some writers see everything as relative), is that we lose any criteria by which to judge that the issues raised by the colour of a person's skin are of much more moral significance than those raised by the colour of a person's front door.

Alister McGrath put it like this:

> To the post-modern suggestion that something can be 'true-for-me' but not 'true', the following reply might be made. Is fascism as equally true as democratic liberalism? Consider the person who believes, passionately and sincerely, that it is an excellent thing to place millions of Jews in gas-chambers. That is certainly 'true-for-him'. But can it be allowed to pass unchallenged? Is it equally true as the belief that one ought to live in peace and tolerance with one's neighbours, including Jews? (McGrath, 1992, p. 227)

One of the finest contemporary moral philosophers who have exposed the failings of the 'modern' world is Alasdair MacIntyre. In his remarkable study *After Virtue*, first published in 1981, he argues that those who speak about morality have lost their way, and what is worse, do not realize that they have done so. He is partly thinking of moral theorists and philosophers, but also of the way in which patterns of moral decision making affect all aspects of our popular culture. Most people, he argues, now think and talk as if emotivism were true, and by 'emotivism' he means the view that all moral judgements are nothing more than the expression of preference, of attitudes or feelings. We are driven by a 'choice' culture. But of course, if that is the case, there is no rational ground for settling moral disagreements between people, such as the example about Nazism we noted just now. We are shut up in a world of moral relativism in which every view is as valid as every other, and questions of truth dissolve into other questions such as psychological effectiveness. He speaks of the bifurcation of the social world into the organizational institutional parts of life, on the one hand, in which values are just assumed but are not discussible, and, on the other hand, into 'the realm of the personal in which judgement and debate about values are central factors, but in which no rational social resolution of issues is available' (MacIntyre, 1981, p. 30). In other words there is a split between the public realm of facts and the private and personal realm of values, and no way across the divide. That is the legacy of modernity.

What is needed is a recovery of what Iris Murdoch in some of her writings called 'deep foundations'. In *The Message to the Planet*, Marcus is talking to Ludens:

> What is sought is not one thing among others, but the foundation of things. Something *necessary*, something which *must* be so ... One must be worthy, and intense purity and refinement of thought is required, even one might say a kind of holiness. (Murdoch, 1990, p. 163)

Our ordinary experience of being aware of moral obligation, or of acting morally, points beyond itself to a transcendent source of goodness. It functions as a signal of transcendence, another glimpse of God.

Another slant on this is found in Charles Taylor's *Ethics of Authenticity*. Reflecting on what he calls the fundamentally 'dialogical' character of human life, he moves on to suggest that when we try to understand our own personal selves, 'we have to take as background some sense of what is significant'. My own feelings cannot *determine* what is significant – that must come from beyond me.

> Even the sense that the significance of my life comes from its being chosen ... depends on the understanding that *independent of my will* there is something, noble, courageous and hence significant in giving shape to my own life. (Taylor, 1991, p. 39)

These philosophers are not reacting to the pressure of modernity by moving into the despair of meaninglessness. They are trying to be post-modern by, in a sense, returning to the premodern acknowledgement that there is an objectivity to our moral awareness, which all of us recognize. This is the argument which forms the basis of C. S. Lewis's early book

The Abolition of Man (1943). The failure to acknowledge a shared moral world leads inevitably to the loss of a great deal of what it means to be human.

There is, therefore, a strong encouragement to Christian people to question the assumption of modernity that morality is something which essentially we invent. On the contrary, it is perfectly coherent and rational to believe in a God who is the source of the moral sense we all know in our deepest selves, a source whose character is most clearly seen in 'demonstrated love'. For 'God so loved the world that he gave his only Son ...' This is not simply a statement of faith for those who like that sort of thing. This is not an expression of personal religious preference. This is a statement about the God who is there and whose love is given to the world, objectively, apart from me, whether I like it or not, whether I receive it or not.

So how does God demonstrate his love? Christian faith affirms that the love of God is supremely demonstrated in the life and death, resurrection and teaching of Jesus. It also teaches that the appropriate response to God's love to us is that we also learn to love.

Love in Jesus

As we have already indicated, the ministry and teaching of Jesus give many examples of self-giving love. To restrict our attention to the Fourth Gospel, there are not only the references in chapter 3 on which this present book is based. In 5.42 he countered his critics for their lack of love; in 8.42 he implies that knowledge of God as Father results in demonstration of love; in 11.5, we read of his particular love for Mary and Martha; in chapters 13–17 he teaches his own disciples about love, particularly in the light of his own demonstration of service through washing their feet; in chapter 21 he calls on Peter to demonstrate his love as a sign of his contrition for betrayal, and his receiving Christ's forgiveness and commission for future service. And the narrative of Jesus' betrayal, trial and death is introduced with the words: 'having loved his own who were in the world, he loved them to the end' (13.1).

If the mission of the Church is to be caught up into the demonstrated love of God seen in Jesus, then we will have to work at ways in which that love is demonstrated in our church life, in the lives of individual Christian members of the Church and in the families and other networks of relationships to which we belong. Much more important than the declaration of doctrine or the preaching of moral rules, important though both of those may be, is the demonstrated love of Christian character.

Love and character

The Fourth Gospel underlines in a variety of ways that people are much more than moral agents. It indicates that the Christian calling and task is to be related to, not just guided by, the moral vision which springs from the love of God. The people we meet are all part of the story that God is telling of his love for the world, and all of us are at different points on our journeys. The Gospel provides a moral vision of a world rooted in the love of God, and expressed in love for one another. It offers a picture of the Christian community which is a school of character building – a place where together we learn what it is to respond to the love of God in Jesus. It centres all human meaning, hopes, values and needs in its understanding of discipleship as allegiance to the one whom Thomas called 'My Lord and my God'.

These are the stories of which Christian morality is made. We hear a great deal about moral values in society, and of course there is much to commend in the task of expressing a shared quest for a shared social morality. But much of the discussion seems often to be at the level of imposing moral rules, about instilling a certain sort of behaviour at school or at home. And of course there is a place for rules and for behavioural control. However, we must beware of reducing morality to moral rules, of reducing people to moral agents, of reducing good character to simply doing the right thing. From the covenant pattern of the Old Testament and from the kingdom values of the New Testament, we learn that biblical ethics is first and foremost not a matter of rules, but of vision, of commitment. Not so much a matter of obeying a moral code as of personal allegiance to a Person. I suggest that the most important thing about a person's morality refers to their basic attitudes towards life and the underlying vision of reality that provides the foundation for those attitudes, the vision and the character which underlie behaviour; how we see the world and how we cope with relationships in it; how we grow the capacities to sustain commitments, offer and receive love, grow to maturity in the journey of faith, become more 'fully alive'. And that is all tied up with the mystery and complexity of the story of a person's on-going journey of faith in relation to Jesus Christ.

Dykstra speaks of Christian ethics as 'visional ethics', and writes,

> Decisions, choices and particular actions are not the first consideration in visional ethics. The foreground is occupied by questions concerning what we see and what it is that enables human beings to see more realistically. For visional ethics, action follows vision; and vision depends on character – a person thinking, reasoning, believing, feeling, willing and acting as a whole. (Dykstra, 1981, p. 36)

The ethics of John derives from his theology. Or, rather, theology and ethics intertwine so closely that they are not really separable (cf. Atkinson, 1993). The whole Gospel presents us with a unified system of values which cannot really be separated from either belief or behaviour.

It will be helpful for us to look first in some detail at John's theological themes. In brief, the history is a record of the self-disclosure of God. The call is to a true discipleship, a being 'born anew', a true worship, a coming to Christ and believing into him, a receiving of his Spirit, being set free by his truth (John 3.7; 4.24; 6.35, 47; 7.39; 8.32). In the well-known 'I am' sayings, Jesus is described as 'the bread of life', 'the light of the world', 'the door of the sheep', 'the good shepherd', 'the resurrection and the life', 'the way, the truth, and the life', 'the true vine' (John 6.35; 8.12; 10.7, 11; 11.25; 14.6; 15.1). John's ethics derives from this conviction about Christ. Christian people are to eat the bread, follow the light, enter the door, know the shepherd, believe in the resurrection, come to the Father through this way, this truth, this life, and abide in Christ the true vine. As E. K. Lee puts it, 'Christian ethics from this point of view are the spontaneous fruit of the true life' (Lee, 1962, p. 238).

And what is the 'true life'? In the Gospel this is partly expressed through signs. The seven signs ('sign' means something that points beyond itself, demonstrating that the living God is at work): water into wine, healing the nobleman's son, healing the lame man, feeding the multitude, walking on the water, healing the man born blind, raising Lazarus (John 2.1–11; 4.46–54; 5.1–18; 6.1–15, 16–21; 9.1–42; 11.1–57). They speak of the authority of Jesus over the natural order, bringing health, refreshment, reassurance, new life.

It is partly expressed through discourses. The seven discourses concern: the new birth, the water of life, the divine Son, the bread of life, the life-giving Spirit, the light of the world, the good shepherd (John 3.1–15; 4.1–42; 5.19–47; 6.22–66; 7.1–52; 8.12–59; 10.1–42).

It is partly worked out in terms of contrasts. First, between the world which God loves and the world which Christ has overcome. Second, between darkness and light: 'I am the light of the world; he who follows me will not walk in darkness, but will have the light of life' (John 1.5; 8.12). Third, between flesh and spirit: flesh means humanity – the Word became flesh (1.14), that which is born of the flesh is flesh (3.6); but Jesus speaks also of a new birth – 'that which is born of the Spirit is spirit', God is spirit (4.24), and the Spirit of God raises fleshly humanity above the earthly level, bringing people into touch with heavenly things (3.12), and so enabling them to worship God in spirit and truth (4.24).

'Sin' is the general Johannine word for humanity's alienation from God. It is a principle of life in this world which manifests itself in unbelief in Christ (cf. 16.9). Jesus' presence brings this unbelief to light, and it is expressed in hatred towards God and hatred towards Jesus (3.16–21). By contrast the new life is described as 'belief in Christ' – or better, 'belief into Christ'. The Gospel was written to bring about this faith (20.31).[2] This is received through believing into him, obeying him, abiding in him, and so coming to know God through him.[3]

One key word summarizes for John the purpose of God in sending his Son to overcome and save the world; that word is love. That one word summarizes the mission of Jesus Christ in obedience to God for the sake of the world; love summarizes the commission of Jesus to his disciples for their continuing life in the world. 'God so loved the world that he gave his only Son, that whoever believes in him should not perish but have eternal life' (John 3.16). 'Jesus ... having loved his own who were in the world ... loved them to the end' (John 13.1, cf 15.9, 13). 'This I command you, to love one another' (John 15.12, 17; cf 17.23).

Love is the central word in Johannine ethics.

Here is a moral vision of the character of loving discipleship which is so much richer than a concentration on moral rules. Part of the task of the mission of the Church is to encourage the long process of building moral vision and character. Some of this will be found within the pastoral and educational ministry of the Church, in the welcome and nurture of believers, in the processes by which discipleship matures.

Love for neighbour – and neighbour-love

If love is the central word in the ethics of the Fourth Gospel, love is also the central word in the teaching of Jesus as reported in the Synoptic Gospels. He summarizes the whole of Christian duty, the whole of 'the law and the prophets' – that is the teaching of (what we call) the Old Testament scriptures – with one text from Deuteronomy:

> You shall love the Lord your God with all your heart and with all your soul and with all your might. (Deuteronomy 6.4)

and one from Leviticus, which is quoted in Matthew (19.19; 22.39) and Mark (12.31, 33), by St Paul (Romans 13.9; Galatians 5.14) and by St James (2.8), who calls it the 'royal law':

You shall love your neighbour as yourself. (Leviticus 19.18)

There is first of all an obligation laid on Christian people to love each other within the Christian fellowship. John's Gospel records Jesus several times saying to his disciples, 'love one another' – this is his new commandment (John 13.34–5; 15.12). The First Letter of John elaborates the theme extensively – Christian brothers and sisters are to love each other. By so doing they abide in the light, they demonstrate that they are children of God, they know that they have passed from death to life. They do so because love is from God, and because God so loved us so we should love each other (1 John 2.10; 3.10, 11, 14, 23; 4.7, 11). Both St Paul and St Peter underline the same point, and urge Christian people to walk in love, to love one another, to love the brotherhood (Romans 13.8, 9, 10; Ephesians 5.2; 1 Peter 1.22; 2.17).

Nor is love merely a sentiment. It is faith in action (Galatians 5.6). The love which is the fruit of the Spirit (Galatians 5.22) involves speaking the truth (Ephesians 4.15), putting up with people we find it hard to like – forbearing (Ephesians 4.2), demonstrating generous concern for social equality (2 Corinthians 8.7, 8, 24). It is expressed in being servants to one another (Galatians 5.13). Servanthood is the hard cash value of neighbour-love. It is typically displayed in kneeling before another's dusty feet with a bowl of water and a towel (John 13.1–17). John 13 begins with a statement of love: 'When Jesus knew that his hour had come ... having loved his own ... he loved them to the end,' and then immediately speaks of service: 'And during supper ... he rose ... laid aside his garments, and girded himself with a towel.' This was how he showed them what discipleship was about: 'If I your Lord and Teacher have washed your feet, you also ought to wash one another's feet.' The mission of the Christian

Church is to be caught up into the mission of Christ, who came among us as one who serves.

But the love and service which ought to characterize the Christian fellowship ought also to characterize a Christian's relationships with all people. St Paul makes no distinction: 'May the Lord make you increase and abound in love *to one another and to all men*' (1 Thessalonians 3.12). Jesus even speaks of the obligation to 'love your enemies' (Matthew 5.44; Luke 6.27, 25). There is no discrimination as to who the appropriate recipients of a Christian's love should be. When Jesus was asked the question: 'And who is my neighbour?', expecting an answer which enabled the questioner to decide whom it was appropriate to love and whom not, Jesus did not answer it. Rather he told a parable – the 'Good Samaritan' (Luke 10.27–36) – not about who a neighbour is, but about the meaning of 'neighbourly love'. The question he answered was not the one he was asked, but the one he himself put back to the questioner: 'Which of these three, do you think, *proved neighbour* to the man who fell among the robbers?' Paul Ramsey quotes Søren Kierkegaard to good effect:

> Christ does not talk about knowing one's neighbour, but about one's self being a neighbour, as the Samaritan proved himself one by his compassion. For by his compassion he did not prove that the man attacked was his neighbour, but that he was the neighbour of the one who was assaulted. (Kierkegaard, 1847, quoted in Ramsey, 1950, p. 93)

The parable, notes Ramsey, tells us something about neighbour-love, nothing about the neighbour. It shows us the nature and meaning of Christian love which discovers the neighbour because it begins with neighbour-love, and not with discriminating between worthy and unworthy people. That is why the heading of this section is not only 'love for neighbour', but more importantly 'neighbour-love'.

Neighbour-love takes very seriously an answer to both the questions posed in these terms by Paul Ramsey: 'What is the good?' but, more importantly, 'Whose good comes first, mine or my neighbour's?' (Ramsey, 1950, p. 114). Neighbour-love shows itself in the creating and the sustaining of human community. It crosses the barriers between enemies. It 'bears all things, believes all things, hopes all things, endures all things. Love never ends' (1 Corinthians 13.7–8). It is the expression of the life and Spirit of Jesus in whom 'all things hold together' (Colossians 1.17). And that fact now takes us into the wider social dimensions of justice.

Love and justice

In social terms, 'the political expression of Love is Justice' (Barry, 1966, p. 217).[4] Much of the morality of the New Testament rests on the basic assumptions about goodness which we find in the Old. As H. H. Rowley summarized Old Testament morality:

> The good life . . . as it is presented to us in the Old Testament is the life that is lived in harmony with God's will and that expresses itself in daily life in the reflection of the character of God translated into the terms of human experience, that draws its inspiration and its strength from communion with God in the fellowship of his people and in private experience, and that knows how to worship and praise him both in public and in the solitude of the heart. (Rowley, 1956, p. 149)

Part of the 'reflection of the character of God . . . into the terms of human experience' is captured by the way some of the prophets, especially those of the eighth century BC, like Amos, Hosea and Micah, call the people of God back to their awareness that they are to be the people of God. In the case of Amos, for example, his main concern was the urgency of the call to justice. It is worth our standing back a little to catch the flavour of Amos' message.

A poor man who lived in the country and dressed sycamore trees, Amos was called to speak the word of God in the kingdom of Israel around 750 BC during the prosperous reign of King Jeroboam II. He worked at an interesting time in Israel's history. Syria was having to give up its military pressure on Israel in order to protect itself from Assyria. In the south, Judah was strong and acted as a buffer state against Egypt. Israel was having a time of political security unknown since the Golden Age of Solomon two hundred years before. Trade and commerce were flourishing. Labour was moving from the land to the cities. There was increasing demand for luxury goods. However, growing self-interest was creating a powerful aristocracy of wealth, and this was leading to the disappearance of what we would call the middle class. There were many things about social life and social institutions which Amos could not take. And he stood out against them.

His first concern was the gap between the rich and the poor and the powerlessness of poverty. The social leaders were living in pride and luxury, but this was leading to the oppression of the poor. 'They sell the righteous for silver, and the needy for a pair of shoes – they that trample the head of the poor into the dust' (Amos 2.6–7).

Second, the social institutions were promoting injustice – the system was actually preventing care from being given to those who needed it. The court in the gate, where justice should have been administered, and where the poor would wait for aid, was no longer the place where justice was done. 'You have turned justice into poison' (6.12).

Third, the religious institutions had themselves become hijacked for political ends. Amos refers to three sacred places, Bethel, Beersheba and Gilgal – places where God had made himself known in the past, holy shrines of the covenant community. Now they had become shrines of the king, secularized and corrupted. God was being manipulated, kept just to a corner of people's concerns. So, says the Lord through Amos: 'Seek me and live; but do not seek Bethel' (5.4–5). The Lord will not hear their praise any more at these corrupt shrines. A community which has become immune to the needs of the poor, has turned a blind eye to oppression, has turned justice into poison and, through the idolization of material prosperity even in the holy places, has cut itself off from the worship of God, has also cut itself off from God's blessing. This is the brunt of Amos' anger.

And the theological basis for his anger is that God is the sovereign of all things – therefore every aspect of life belongs to God; God's holy and just character stands behind his call for righteousness and justice among the people; human beings are precious to God – there is a shared common humanity to which Amos can appeal. Justice, in other words, is for people. This is why he cries out: 'Let justice roll down like waters, and righteousness like an ever-flowing stream' (5.24).

For Amos, justice is the justice of God – a justice which is much more than just civic fairness. God's justice merges into righteousness and goodness on the one side, and into mercy and redemption on the other. God's justice is not static, but dynamic – transformative and redemptive. Justice is included in the sort of love which gives.

I believe it was George MacDonald who said, 'Man is not made only for justice from his fellows, but for love, which is greater than justice and by including, supersedes it.' Here is a justice which is the social and political expression of love. God's justice transforms human conceptions of justice, motivating us to move nearer to his justice in our human societies.

Amos had very little political success. Samaria the capital eventually fell to invaders and the kingdom of Israel was dismantled. But he stood in the breach at a crucial time and bore witness to his God. Christian mission, likewise, bears witness to the love and justice of God. Christian mission, caught up into the mission of God, finds ways of demonstrating love and justice in our world.

Love through politics

How is love expressed in government, national and local, and in the practice of politics? Such a question raises prior questions about the theology of politics and therefore about the nature of humanity and the values on which human community depends: love and justice, liberty and equality.

The history of the Church shows that it cannot be taken for granted that the issues of politics and the love of God can be spoken of in the same breath. In fact, we find an ambiguous relationship between Christian faith and political ideas: sometimes partners, sometimes opponents. There is no space here to explore these themes in any detail,[5] but at different times The State has been viewed as both good and bad in relation to the Church's view of God's world. Likewise, the Church itself as an institution has exercised political influence for good and for ill.

This is, of course, a vast field. We will concentrate simply on three political values: humanity, community and social justice.

Humanity

Stanley Jaki wrote a book called *Angels, Apes and Men* (1983) in which he argued that to do justice to the full meaning of what it is to be human we need to avoid the idealism that suggests we are really embodied angels, and the reductionism that suggests we are only self-conscious apes. Neither reductionism nor self-deification are consistent with a Christian theology, but nor, I think, are they consistent with our experience of what it is to be human. Our experience is one of ambiguity. We are able look at ourselves, analyse and discuss ourselves in all our physical make-up; and we are also able to come round the other side of the camera and recognize all sorts of ways in which our spiritual nature transcends our physical make-up.

As Blaise Pascal put it in his extravagant way in the seventeenth century:

> It is dangerous to explain too clearly to man how like he is to the animals without pointing out his greatness. It is also dangerous to make too much of his greatness without his vileness. It is still more dangerous to leave him in ignorance of both ... Man must not be allowed to believe that he is equal either to animals or angels. (Pascal, 1670)

Pascal knew that the ambiguity extends to the moral area of life also. We aim so high, but often fall so low. 'I do not do the good I want, but the evil I do not want is what I do (Romans

7.19). There is, in other words, the need for an understanding not only of the wonder of the fact that human beings are created to bear the image of God, but also of the fact of sin. This ambiguity means that in our human interrelationships, we need a political realism.

We may not treat ourselves only in terms of the thorough-going optimistic idealism of human nature which we find, for example, at times in that theorist of democracy, Jean-Jacques Rousseau. At the beginning of his *Social Contract* (1762), he writes: 'Man is born free, but everywhere he is in chains.' In other places, Rousseau blames most of human unhappiness and social friction not on the individual, but on society and social structures.

Nor may we operate only in terms of the thoroughgoing empiricist pessimism of human nature which we seem to find in Thomas Hobbes' insistence on the absolute need of government, and who writes about every human's desire to preserve his own liberty and acquire dominion over others. 'Both these desires are dictated by the impulse to self-preservation. From their conflict arises a war of all against all – which makes life nasty, brutish and short' (Hobbes, 1651). Government for Hobbes is an essential protection against the state of nature.

A theological realism needs to come to terms with the paradox and the ambiguity, with our earthiness and our spirituality, our creativity in God's image, and our sin, and to structure our relationships in the light of it. Our politics needs to take this ambiguity seriously without over-optimism about our autonomous capacity to be good outside the help of God's grace, and without over-pessimism about human short-comings. Reinhold Niebuhr's defence of democracy got it exactly right: 'Man's capacity for justice makes democracy possible; but man's inclination to injustice makes democracy necessary' (Niebuhr, 1945, p. vi).

One crucial theological contribution to politics is a perspective on what it is to be human – to affirm our preciousness as people made in the image of God, and the marring of that image through sin.

Human community

Shirley Williams in her book *Politics is for People* comments on the way Robert Owen and R. H. Tawney saw that 'the industrial revolution had torn apart organic feudal society and replaced the Christian concept of the whole man with the abstraction of economic man' (Williams, 1981, p. 24). She argues that the socialist politics she stands for is not primarily about public ownership or state control of the economy, it is about fellowship, community and participation.

One of the legacies of the Enlightenment in Western Europe in the last two hundred years has been the emergence of 'the individual'. As we shall argue more fully in our next chapter, if we human beings are to be the image of God, then for us to be truly human means that we are essentially persons in relation to other persons. We are, to use the Old Testament word, in covenants.

The Chief Rabbi Jonathan Sacks draws on the Old Testament concept of covenant in his discussion of democracy (Sacks, 1995, p. 109). 'Covenant' holds together the sense of corporate solidarity of a people bound together with ties of mutual promise and obligation, while not losing the importance of individual freedom, choice and responsibility. In the Old Testament, the divine covenant is used again and again as a paradigm for our human covenants which we make with one another: wife/husband, parent/child, teacher/pupil, political leader/constituent, neighbour/neighbour. When our human covenants are shaped by the divine covenant, they make for the best of human flourishing. Despite the exegetical problems raised concerning covenant in Old Testament scholarship, the concept still seems to be to provide an illuminating and creative way of characterizing human relationships and human communities.

Covenant is more than contract. Covenant is a dynamic relationship between parties based on commitment and consent. It is about mutuality not coercion. It is about the priority of human values over material values. At its heart are words like communion; service; stewardship; forgiveness; and a priority towards those who are disadvantaged – in other words, demonstrated neighbour-love.

Social justice

There are many different ways of understanding the word 'justice'. For some people, justice means fairness, everybody getting a fair deal. For other people, justice includes the idea of human rights. But what are human rights?

At the heart of the covenant faith of the Jews which was taken up into Christianity, is the giving of God's law, Torah – God's loving instructions. But Torah does not stand alone as a detached legal code. It is given within the wider framework of a covenant of grace. Its purpose, then, is relational. We are most familiar with the Ten Commandments, which may well have functioned as part of ancient Israel's criminal law (Philipps, 1970), but they also served as a reminder of the basic moral values which undergird a covenantal society, because they reflect something of the moral character of God. They are picked up as a framework for the Sermon on the Mount in the Gospel, and for some of the writings of St Paul. If we are going to use the language of human rights, we need to relate this to God's Torah, because if we are going to talk about human rights, the covenant model requires us also to talk about human responsibilities. This is to root human rights further back than John Locke did, or Tom Paine did, in their political theories (cf. Locke, 1690; Paine, 1791). They suggest that human rights are something to do with individual autonomy, individual freedom and individual choice. But if our rights as human beings are related to the fact that we are made in the divine image, and our relationships are most fulfilling if they reflect the divine covenant, then there is an essential mutuality of rights and responsibilities.

At the risk of oversimplification, we can use the Decalogue (Exodus 20.1–17; Deuteronomy 5.6–21) as a summary of God's loving instructions for covenanted human responsibilities; that is, for how people are to live responsibly if their lives are to be fulfilled and their society is to function healthily. From the teaching of Jesus Christ, we learn that God's Torah can be summarized in two brief statements: love towards God, and love towards other human beings.

The section of the Decalogue corresponding with love towards God includes commandments about honouring God's name and keeping a day for worship. This suggests that we may speak of a basic right to assemble for worship without interference. The section corresponding with love towards other human beings includes a commandment against murder, which implies a basic right to life, and the responsibility to respect another person's life, and to see that innocent human beings should not be deliberately killed. It includes a commandment against adultery, which implies a basic right to expect faithfulness, and a responsibility on society to uphold the value of marriage and family. It includes a commandment against stealing, which implies a basic right for people to own what is rightfully theirs, and a responsibility to uphold the value of other people's property. It includes a commandment against bearing false witness against another human being, which implies a basic right to an honest reputation, and a responsibility to ensure that society is built on truth and not on deceit.

Underneath all these, there are basic sustenance rights, for example rights to sufficient food and shelter. Yet we all know that in the modern world, our share in the resources which are available to sustain life are in large measure related to the social and economic structures which our nation states adopt, and which the world economic structures dictate. They are also increasingly related to the global questions about the sustainability of any life at all on this planet, and to our stewardship of the environment in which we live. There are pressing Christian concerns here, in the context of world hunger and world energy needs, and the world's future, which bring God's justice onto an international agenda.

Finally we need to say something more about the justice of God. In the Bible, God is described as just.[6] His justice is then used as a standard by which human justice is measured. But God's justice goes beyond what human justice requires – God's justice merges into goodness and into mercy. God's justice includes provision for the needy, punishment for the wrong-doer, the offer of forgiveness for the penitent, comfort for the suffering, health for the sick, and what has been called 'a bias' on behalf of the poor, the disadvantaged and the outcasts – in other words, a concern for human welfare and well-being at all levels.

The biblical word which captures this sense of well-being based on the justice of God is shalom (cf. Atkinson, 1985, ch. 9). Often translated 'peace', shalom means much more than the absence of conflict. Shalom based on justice is present when people enjoy good relationships with each other, within their communities, throughout their land and with their God. There is a personal and a social dimension to shalom. The prophet Jeremiah even urges the leaders of the people of God who had been taken off into exile in Babylon: 'Seek the welfare [shalom] of the city where I have sent you into exile, and pray to the Lord on its behalf, for in its welfare you will find your welfare' (Jeremiah 29.7).

There is not space here to treat the complicated questions of freedoms and benefits, of punishment and law enforcement, of criminal justice and the relationships of offenders and society. But enough has been said to demonstrate that politics which is for people is also for justice between people. The mission of the Church has inescapably to be caught up into the political process and bear its witness within the political process. For it is here that more clearly than anywhere else we seek to demonstrate that social justice is the political expression of neighbour-love.

Love is at the heart of the mission of God. Love was demonstrated, in that 'God so loved . . . that he gave'. Love was demonstrated in the life, teaching, ministry, death and resurrection of Jesus Christ. Love is now to be demonstrated through the mission of the Church, caught up into the love of God, bearing witness to Jesus Christ. That demonstration includes love through the Christian character of individual and community life; it includes the expression of love for neighbour in personal relationships; and it includes the quest for justice in all human affairs.

Chapter 5

HIS ONLY SON

Mission, we have said, means God's mission. If we are going to say anything about the mission of the Church, I believe it needs to be said in this context: mission means God's mission – the outflowing of the life and love of God towards the world. And that is crucially focused in Jesus Christ, to whom our key text refers: his only Son.

In turning our attention to Jesus Christ, I want to have in mind the third major section of our discussion of modernity and post-modernity, namely what I earlier called social patterns. It may seem rather a long leap from a text about Jesus Christ to a discussion of social patterns of the post-Enlightenment world, but what I hope I demonstrated in our introductory chapter is that it was precisely a changed emphasis on what it means to be human – a new emphasis on the individual rather than on the centrality of interpersonal relationships, that contributed to those changed social patterns dominated by individualism or its flip-side, totalitarianism. 'What is it to be a person?' is the question which underlies much of the debates in post-modernity. Clearly that is a question, as with so many we have touched on, which demands a whole book on its own. But we will explore the centrality of Jesus Christ in our text with these questions in mind, and holding also to the mission implications of our conclusions.

We begin with a brief glance at the way Jesus' death and resurrection are the climax of the story of his life; then at the New Testament emphasis on Jesus as 'Lord'; and finally at the Trinitarian implications of saying that Jesus is 'his Son' – and what that says to us about persons-in-relation.

Jesus Christ: the clearest glimpse of God

The testimony of the New Testament is that Jesus Christ is the fullest and clearest glimpse of God within our world and our history. Many books have been written about the historical Jesus, and every now and then another seeks to demonstrate that either he did not exist, or did not die, or did not rise from the dead, or that some aspect or other of the New Testament witness is unreliable. But he still continues to exercise an influence and fascination over countless mlllions of people's minds and hearts. And for every book of sceptical popularism, there is another of responsible scholarship demonstrating the reliability of the New Testament witness.[1] Jesus, the first-century Jew, is presented to us as one in whom the hopes and aspirations of the contemporary Jewish religion came to their fulfilment.

Jesus announces the fulfilment of the hopes and longings of God's people, and especially that fulfilment in himself. In him God's kingdom is present – not as a revolutionary political movement, but as the establishment of the reign of God in the world and in people's lives. His healing ministry crosses barriers of taboo (he touches the leper and the dead body) to include the outcasts, the unwelcome, the poor, the unwanted within the embrace of God's love. His teaching ministry exposes the failures of human sinfulness and the need for divine grace to enable God's kingdom of love and justice to come 'on earth as it is in heaven'. As we shall elaborate in Chapter 7, his death demonstrates the entry of God into the darkest of human pain and alienation, and his resurrection displays the triumph of life over death, good over evil, love over hatred, and the kingdom of God over all dehumanizing and destructive powers. His gift of the Holy Spirit and the promise of his presence is the life and meaning of the Christian Church, which began with a small band of fearful disciples, shut in a room in Jerusalem behind locked doors, which within a generation had become a significant force throughout the Mediterranean world, and within decades had effectively come to dominate the thought world of the Roman empire. Faith in Jesus Christ has inspired the art, architecture, legal systems, literature, music and social patterns of much of the Western world, and is now growing at an unprecedented rate in Latin America, Africa and South East Asia.

The life and significance of one Galilean carpenter who lived a short 33 years in a tiny province of the first-century Roman empire points beyond itself to the God he named as 'Father'.

The mission of the Christian Church is to bear witness to the God who is made known in Jesus Christ; to share in the Spirit in the life of Jesus Christ; to display in our lives and communities the character of Jesus Christ; to help one another as disciples to follow Jesus Christ – the human being who is fully alive.

But central to the Gospel presentation of Jesus is his death and resurrection. The text we have chosen as our theme text ('God so loved the world that he gave his only Son, that whoever believes in him should not perish but have eternal life') comes in the Fourth Gospel immediately after a reference to Jesus' death. 'As Moses lifted up the serpent in the wilderness' – a reference to a moment of healing in the place of disease and death during the Exodus events (Numbers 21.9) – 'so must the Son of man be lifted up.' This lifting up of the Son of man is the author's figurative way of speaking of the exaltation to glory of the Son of man, but in John's Gospel, that exaltation is seen in the very specific lifting up of Jesus on the cross (cf. John 12.32–3) – a death which is understood in the Gospel only from the perspective of the resurrection. So what, for our author, is the significance of the death and resurrection of Jesus?

We need to get our bearings again in first-century Judaism, and try to understand how the New Testament presents the history of the death and resurrection of Jesus in that context. Tom Wright[2] summarizes an understanding of the history of Jesus' death with these three themes.[3] First, Jesus warned his contemporaries of imminent divine judgement. The teaching and ministry of the kingdom which the Gospels narrate is indeed about the expectation that God would come. God would come in judgement (as the action of cleansing the temple symbolized). He would come to remove evil and to establish shalom (as the exorcisms and healings indicate). Jesus was summoning into being a renewed covenant people of God, to be the true Israel, to live the life of God's kingdom in justice, righteousness and shalom. He was summoning into being a renewed people of God, namely those who follow him as the focus of true Israel.

Second, Jesus did not merely proclaim judgement against the people of God, he identified himself with Israel. When Jesus warned negatively of judgement, he also positively summoned disciples to follow him, to be part of the renewed people of God he was calling into being. Just as Israel in the Old Testament is the representative of all humanity – is a light to all the nations – so Jesus who presents himself as Israel, becomes the representative human being.

Third, Jesus, as Israel's representative, took upon himself the judgement which he pronounced against the nation. In his death, we see the judgement of God against all that does not display the true nature of God's kingdom, is not in line with God's justice, righteousness and shalom. In his resurrection, there is a coming into being of a reconstituted humanity. Here is the true Israel of God, on its way to the kingdom of God's glory.

What these themes imply for our experience and our living, is a task we will explore more fully in Chapter 7 of this book.

We need to underline, however, the phrase which St Paul uses to summarize his discussion about the way God reconciles the world to himself and brings about a new creation: 'All this is from God' (2 Corinthians 5.18). The benefits of the life, death and resurrection of Jesus in the creation of a new humanity which is on its way to the kingdom of God's glory, in which all of creation is healed and all humanity comes fully alive, is all of God's gift, born of his love. It was because God so loved the world that he gave his only Son.

We turn now to another New Testament phrase used to describe Jesus Christ – the Lord.

'Jesus Christ is Lord'

When I was a student and my wife was earning the money we took a student charter flight to Rome. We visited some catacombs, caves under the north of the city, cut out of the soft volcanic rock, where we were shown drawings on the sides of the caves depicting a cross, a fish – signs from the early Christians who used to worship there at the time when they were persecuted by the Roman emperor. We were told, whether it is true or not I do not know – I suspect our guide was several decades out in his story-telling – that it was in these caves that people in the earliest Christian communities used to say to one another, perhaps as a word of encouragement, perhaps as a baptismal creed: 'Jesus is Lord.' Whether or not our guide was right, that phrase certainly found its way as an early credal statement into the pages of the New Testament, and made its own imprint on the shape of Christian mission.

If we are to explore the shape of Christian mission, I believe we need to set our compass bearings from this phrase: Jesus is Lord.

Care is needed, because the language of lordship is rather uncomfortable today, and not only for those properly sensitized to inclusive language, and for whom the word 'lord' has echoes of patriarchy and chauvinism. What do we think of when we use the word 'lord'? Perhaps the House of Lords? It is not always obvious how to make a direct link between the House of Lords and the kingdom of God. Perhaps we think of 'lordliness', as in Shakespeare's line about 'pages and footboys who dance attendance on their lordship's pleasures'. Perhaps we are embarrassed because to speak of Jesus as Lord in a multi-ethnic, multi-faith culture sounds too much like the Christian imperialism of nineteenth-century missionary movements, when becoming a Christian was almost equivalent to serving the British empire. Or perhaps in our post-modern culture we discover that the language of 'lord' sounds rather too much like a claim to public truth, whereas religion – we are told, as we have said before – can apparently only be concerned with private opinion and personal preference.

But this is to miss what the New Testament phrase 'Jesus is Lord' is about. It is not about patriarchy or political power, or domineering lordliness, or imperialistic evangelism or private opinion. It is about the way God is; it *is* about public truth. It is, I believe, the light in which we see light. But it requires some semantic redirection. There is, as we shall see, something subversive about the way Paul uses it. We need to be aware that 'lord' is never used of Jesus in the New Testament as an example of domination and oppression. We need to find a way of re-appropriating the word to express for us what it meant for Paul.

One of the places in which St Paul uses the phrase is in the hymn which we now have as part of Philippians chapter 2: 'every tongue confess that Jesus Christ is Lord'. Paul is writing to Christians in Philippi – a small city in Macedonia, a centre of commerce and trade, a place of much variety, multi-ethnic and multi-faith. There were many gods on offer in Philippi and the one of whom the word 'lord' was used most especially was the Roman emperor. So when St Paul says 'Jesus is Lord' he is not just using a polite term of respect, he is unmistakably setting Jesus in the centre of his concern for a city which had many gods, some very dehumanizing. He is also being politically subversive in referring to Jesus with a word used of the Roman emperor.

As in Philippi, our culture is given over to the worship of other gods – some of which are dehumanizing. The trust some still place in nuclear deterrence is one example. The worship of the market economy is another, creating increasing social alienation and injustice. The British mystery religion called the National Lottery might be yet a third. Bureaucracy and technology can both be good servants; they can also become the iron cages of alien lords. We, too, have many gods, so Paul may have a word for us.

In this paragraph (Philippians 2.5–13) Paul takes us on a theological journey which we need to follow. He says to a divided and quarrelling church in Philippi: Have this mind among yourselves which you have in Christ, who though he was in God's image did not use his equality with God to his own advantage.

Paul is, I think, drawing a contrast between Adam and Christ. In the Genesis story, Adam was disobedient; in the New Testament story, Jesus was obedient. Adam grasped at a life which was not his; Jesus did not use what he had to his own

advantage, but gave his life away as a servant of others. Adam
stands for people alienated from God, from each other, from
their environment, within themselves. Adam is humanness
gone awry. Jesus is the true human being in the image of
God, who takes on Adam's world; its guilt, shame, fear,
injustice, even death on a cross. Therefore, we are told, God
has highly exalted him.

Paul's argument is this: the resurrection and exaltation of
Jesus are God's way of saying that when Jesus enters the world
of other gods, their power is broken. Jesus is the true human
being. It is also a way of saying that what Jesus is, God is. God
is the sort of God who gives himself away for the sake of others,
a God who is engaged in the earthiness of our humanity, even
to the Cross.

This is why Jesus is given the name 'Lord'. We are offered
the vision of the crucified and risen Christ breaking through
dehumanizing powers, in heaven and on earth and under the
earth, and taking the life of authentic, vibrant, exalted
humanness right into God himself. The Athanasian creed,
that early statement of Christian faith, includes a remarkable
phrase. It speaks of Jesus Christ 'taking manhood into God'.
Jesus took humanity into God.

Furthermore, the testimony of Christian faith is that, by our
union with Jesus Christ – that is by our life in his Spirit of life –
we too can be 'taken into God'. That is what I think this
sentence means, with the wonderful imagery of the end-time,
'in the name of Jesus' – as we may translate this verse – 'every
knee shall bow to the glory of God the Father' (Philippians
2.10). Every person who lives in the name – that is through the
mediation – of Jesus Christ is brought into the worship the
whole of creation offers to God the Father.

This phrase also has unmistakable echoes of Isaiah 45.23.
There the prophet is speaking about the salvation of the
gentiles by the God of Israel, and the coming of all nations
to worship the one true God, and that this is the glory of Israel
itself, the purpose for which Israel was chosen by God (Isaiah
42.6). The old moulds will be broken (Isaiah 45.9), and
glorious new things will happen. The time will come when

the people of God will no longer be defined by their national identity, but by their confession of faith in the one true God.

> There is no other god besides me, a righteous God and a Saviour; there is none besides me. Turn to me and be saved, all the ends of the earth! For I am God, and there is no other. By myself I have sworn, from my mouth has gone forth in righteousness a word that shall not return: 'To me every knee shall bow, every tongue shall swear.' (Isaiah 45.21–3)

This language about the worship of the one true God in whom all people find their salvation is now used by St Paul to speak of Jesus.

In the development of the picture of the Servant of the Lord in these chapters in Isaiah, we see a Servant who comes to stand for the whole people of Israel, and – since Israel in a sense represents all the nations, and is called to be a light to the nations – who also therefore stands for all humanity. The Servant of the Lord is what God intended all humanity to be. The New Testament presents Jesus as the representative human being. In other words, Jesus is the way, throughout our uncertain pilgrimage journey, that we too may become authentically human. This I think is what Paul means when he says Jesus, the servant, is Jesus the Lord. Jesus Christ is, so to speak, God's mission statement.

Have we not now reached the heart of the mission of God, and of our mission as being caught up into the life and love of God for the sake of the world? The heart of mission is the love we see in the self-giving of Jesus the servant Lord – in both incarnation and resurrection, both participation and transformation, both presence and liberation. This is the shape of God's mission. It places the cross and resurrection of Jesus at the centre of all things.

It is a celebration of God's confrontation with and breaking through all dehumanizing powers.

It is a celebration of what it means to be a true human being, caught up into the worship of God the Father. As Irenaeus put it: 'The glory of God is a human being fully alive.'

It gives us a vision of a way in which we – with people of all races and all places – can discover our true selves by being taken up into the life of God.

This is wonderfully transforming and recreative good news, if we can but see it. This is a light by which we can see all things new, by which creation can be healed. So where does all this take us? To adapt Bonhoeffer's question: Who is Jesus Christ for us today? What are the implications for the mission of the Christian Church in the contemporary world?

- To say Jesus is Lord calls in question our allegiance to all other gods.
- To say Jesus is Lord is to speak the language of the kingdom which is present personally in Jesus, but is still to be prayed for, worked at and lived out through the struggling journeys of our lives. This is a vision which draws us forward: there is a 'not yet' which energizes and mobilizes us now.
- To say Jesus is Lord has implications for church life. It was to a divided and quarrelling Philippian church that Paul wrote: Have this mind among yourselves which you have in Christ Jesus, who emptied himself, taking the form of a servant. This is the unifying, ecumenical dimension of mission.
- To say Jesus is Lord, the language of the kingdom, has political implications for public life. This is why Paul has earlier said: Live worthily of the gospel as citizens (Philippians 1.27). There is a political subversiveness to an alternative lifestyle shaped by the Gospel.
- To say Jesus is Lord of all has implications for other faiths. Although we cannot simply say that all religions are different forms of the same thing, nor can we trap Jesus the Lord within the bounds of the Christian Church, or within a particular dogmatic code. The Spirit of life of the living Lord is alive and well outside our Church and beyond our ways of speaking of him.[4]
- To use the language of God's kingdom has implications for the way we treat God's world: other races, other people, other animals, other environments. It commits us to justice

between people, and to the welfare of our and our children's ecological home.

Paul's word to the Church in Philippi seems apt for us: Let this mind be among yourselves which you have in Christ Jesus. Let the Church – and its institutions – be marked by giving itself away in love for the sake of others. As David Bosch put it, 'mission is the church crossing frontiers in the form of a servant' (Bosch, 1992). But let it also be marked by that central allegiance to the One in whose light we see everything else; whose light we are called to reflect in the world. That central allegiance of which Paul speaks when he says of himself: 'I count everything as loss because of the surpassing worth of knowing Christ Jesus my Lord' (Philippians 3.8).

Persons in relation

To turn, now, to the third theme of this chapter, we note again that in Jesus' resurrection, there is a reconstituted *humanity*. In the text in Philippians we have just been considering, the call is for a *corporate* response: have this mind among yourselves which you have in Christ Jesus. Our theme is persons in *relation*.

One of the assumptions being made by the writer of the Fourth Gospel is that Jesus Christ is properly called God's 'only Son'. In other words, in God himself, there are, so to speak, family relationships. Or to put it in the language of the doctrine of the Holy Trinity – God is 'persons in relationship'.

We have earlier mentioned how central a feature of modernity is the stress on the individual. In some respects, 'the individual' was invented at the time of the Enlightenment in Western Europe. By contrast, many non-Western cultures today – as with the biblical cultures of the past – have a much more social understanding of what it is to be human than the excessive individualism of our modern Western world, summarized in the statement attributed to Margaret Thatcher: 'There is no such thing as society.'

Now I do not wish to be misunderstood here. Of course the individual is important. The text in John's Gospel speaks of

'whoever' believes in him. People are given their individual
names at birth, and their individual names at baptism.
Everyone matters to God and is valued by God and known
by God. The Good Shepherd, we are told, knows his sheep.
Our Father in heaven knows when every sparrow falls to the
ground. St Paul speaks of Jesus as 'my' Lord. However, we are
born into a network of human relationships – and these can
either facilitate growth towards maturity, or get in the way.
We have already commented on the perspective of Jesus Christ
as the embodiment of a new humanity. In the Old Testament,
the individual and the corporate belong inextricably together.
The covenant community holds together the individual person
and also their wider social group – even sometimes in a sort of
corporate person. In the New Testament, believers who are
baptized individually (though sometimes as part of house-
holds), and whose baptism is a reminder that God's covenant
promises are now made especially to them, at the same time
become part of the baptized body of Christ and family of God.
There is an essentially corporate dimension to biblical understandings of what it is to be a person – which are a long way
from the individualism of Enlightenment Europe.

The extent to which we see ourselves either as individuals or
as persons in relationship will determine to some extent how we
treat one another in God's world.

Here is a famous passage from the Jewish philosopher
Martin Buber:

> The world is twofold for man in accordance with his twofold
> attitude.
>
> The attitude of man is twofold in accordance with the two
> basic words he can speak.
>
> The basic words are not single words, but word-pairs.
>
> One basic word is the word-pair 'I-You'.
>
> The other basic word is the word-pair 'I-It'; but this basic
> word is not changed when He or She takes the place of It.
>
> Thus the I of man is also twofold. For the I of the basic
> word 'I-You' is different from that in the basic word 'I-It'.
>
> When I confront a human being as my You and speak the

basic word 'I-You' to him, then he is not a thing among things nor does he consist of things …

Even as a melody is not composed of tones, nor a verse of words, nor a statue of lines – one must pull and tear to turn a unity into a multiplicity – so it is with the human being to whom I say 'I-You'. I can abstract from him the colour of his hair or the colour of his speech or the colour of his graciousness; I have to do this again and again; but immediately he is no longer You. (Buber, 1970, p. 53)

The Scottish philosopher John Macmurray said a similar thing:

The Self exists only in dynamic relation with the Other … the Self is constituted by its relation to the Other; … it has its being in its relationship; … this relationship is necessarily personal. (Macmurray, 1961, p. 17)

The same point was made, we recall, from a completely different standpoint by the Dutch theologian Heije Faber. He emphasized how much psychoanalytic theory takes very seriously the importance of relationships early in life, and then interpreted this in the light of Christian theology. 'The sacred mystery already proclaims itself in the infantile bond, and … where normal, this develops into a mature relationship with God' (Faber, 1976, p. 241). In other words, the mystery of human interrelationships is so significant, precisely because they reflect something of the fact that the heart of the universe (God) is relational.

What are we to make of this?

From our Christian understanding of God as a Holy Trinity of Persons in personal communion – which means that the heart of this universe is persons in relation – these philosophers are absolutely correct to criticize some aspects of the culture we have inherited from the Enlightenment. From René Descartes onwards, we have learned to see ourselves as isolated individuals, operating largely with a rational system of natural causes. We see ourselves as autonomous, individualized centres of consciousness. From David Hume we learned to be sceptical about anything supernatural. From Immanuel Kant we learned to separate the empirical world of facts from the spiritual world of values. All this has led us to believe that 'facts' are public, observable, objective, whereas 'values' are matters of private preference and individual choice.

This view of ourselves necessarily affects the way we think of ourselves and our relationships. Combining this Enlightenment heritage with sophisticated technology, we can now see ourselves mostly as constructionists, interveners in the system, manipulators. What matters is technique, problem-solving, not relating. The ideal becomes detachment not engagement, autonomy not mutual interdependence. We see the world mostly as 'I-It', and this crowds out more personal ways of living: 'I-You'.

The results are well known, and have been well described by Colin Gunton in *Enlightenment and Alienation* (1985). People become alienated from each other. We become alienated from our environment. We become divided up within ourselves. Down the deep fissures which open up in our culture go words like 'purpose', 'meaning', 'community', 'fellowship', 'society'. We become like the picture described in C. S. Lewis's novel *The Great Divorce* in which hell is depicted as a city in which everyone is always moving out.

The economic and bureaucratic structures of the modern world also play their part in crushing the personal. It is at this point that Max Weber's phrase 'the iron cage' becomes so telling. In the early twentieth century he wrote his controversial *The Protestant Ethic and the Spirit of Capitalism* (1992, first published 1920), in which he commented on the way what he thought of as the Puritan (such as Richard Baxter's) understanding of work as a calling gave way to 'the tremendous cosmos of the modern economic order'. He continues:

> This order is now bound to the technical and economic conditions of machine production which today determine the lives of all the individuals who are born into this mechanism, not only those directly concerned with economic

acquisition, with irresistible force. Perhaps it will so determine them until the last ton of fossilised coal is burnt. In
Baxter's view the care for external goods should only lie on
the shoulders of the 'saint like a light cloak, which can be
thrown aside at any moment'. But fate decreed that the
cloak should become an iron cage. (Weber, 1992, p. 181)

Important as the individual is, the individualism of this part of
the Enlightenment heritage is not true to the world as it is. We
are coming to see all too clearly that the loss of the sense of
community very quickly leads to the loss of personal significance for people. Similarly, we are seeing that there are
'problems' in human life and society for which there are no
techniques, no solutions. We are being forced on all sides to re-
examine this aspect of the Enlightenment framework of understanding. We are forced back to other models of personal
interrelationship in which our modes of interaction are communion rather than technique.

The biblical picture of the covenant relationship of God
with the people of Israel, which is an analogy for the sorts of
interpersonal relationships which make for the best for human
flourishing, starts from the fact that we are not essentially
autonomous and separate individuals, but are, in the root of
our being, persons in relation.

We need to be particularly sensitive how we express this in
relation to people at the edges of life (the very young or the
very old) who are incapable of sustaining what we normally
think of as personal relationships, or those whose illness traps
them within a world of their own, or makes interpersonal
relating extremely hard. We are not so much talking about
the quality of a person's relationships as the fact that each
person is necessarily part of a network of personal relating –
which may be health-giving (a covenant of care) or destructive. Clearly also such covenants of care are not always
mutually supportive. A person may find that they are contrib-
uting much more care and attention than they are receiving
when they are a parent with a young baby. As the baby grows
to maturity, the relationship becomes much more equal and

co-operative. Later in life the erstwhile baby becomes the adult caring for the elderly parent. Yet through this rhythm of mutuality, individual personal identity is intimately linked with covenant belonging. And where that is missing, humanity is diminished. To adapt the title of John Zizioulas' book (1985), Being *is* Communion.

In one sense, the whole of the book of Hosea is effectively an exposition of this theme. It begins with the acted parable of Hosea's family situation which is then elaborated as an analogy of God's covenant relationship with the people of Israel. The heart of the message is the meaning of love in relationship – a love which is offered in spite of unfaithfulness, a love which forgives and seeks a restoration of fellowship.

In the New Testament, the affirmation that Jesus Christ is Lord is coupled with an exposition of the Church as the body of Christ, in which every member belongs, and in which each has gifts and each has needs, and which 'when each part is working properly, makes bodily growth and upbuilds itself in love' (Ephesians 4.16).

The tremendous importance of this for the mission of the Church is that it touches on what it means to be human. If I am who I am only in relation to you, and you are who you are only in relation to me, to your parents, to your colleagues, to your friends, to your society, to your God, it is vital that the Church engages with those features of our culture which push us apart, make us separate, destroy communion and fellowship and belonging. We are all set in a network of relationships. If it is the case that we grow into full humanity by loving and being loved, and so become really and truly ourselves, a major part of our mission will be to seek to create and sustain community in a world in which many forces are working in the opposite direction.

This will find expression in the Church's pattern of pastoral care. It will be seen in the house groups, cells, after-church gatherings, midweek fellowships, organizations and so on which make up church life. It will be seen as the church community sees itself as a therapeutic community in which each has gifts and each has needs. It will be seen as the Church learns to be a community of character building, and through the mutual accountability of one to another, people grow in maturity of character, in showing the fruit of God's spirit in love, joy and peace.

But it will also show, and this is less easy to maintain, in the local church's commitment to its local neighbourhood and community. There is a great deal of Christian ethics written about personal matters like sex, and about global matters like war. There is much less about what it means to create and maintain a sense of community in the inner city, about what it means to develop co-operative ways of handling commerce, about a theology of the local bus service and the local unemployment register. How is the Church creating community for those who are homeless, or the victims of racial violence on our streets? How is it maintaining community in those villages without public transport and where you have to travel to the local town to meet all the professional carers, except perhaps the vicar who has six such villages in his parish. Safety for children's play, awareness of the presence of sex offenders released back into the neighbourhood, the values expressed by the local newspaper, the priorities for the governing body of the local school, the provision of care for local elderly people, the management of the neighbours nobody likes. These and a thousand other examples are the touchstone of what Christian community development is about. They are part of the mission of God. It is in *this* world that we work out the implications of the faith that Jesus is Lord.

God the Holy Trinity is in God's own self a communion of persons in relationships of love in which the creator Father, redeemer Son and sanctifying Spirit give themselves to each other in love and from whose creative love all things come. The Scriptures tell us that we human beings are in the image of God; then for us to be truly human means that we are intended to be persons in relation to other persons, and essentially in relation to God's own self. And that is both gift and task. It is gift – because we are made in God's image. It is task because we are called through grace to grow and to help one another to grow into God's likeness, into what the New Testament calls 'the measure of the stature of the fullness of Christ' (Ephesians 4.13).

To be human, then, is to be united with Jesus Christ the Lord, through the Spirit, and in him to be drawn into the love of God, and become more fully alive.

Intriguingly, the language of post-modern science, particularly in chaos theory and in complexity theory, to which we briefly referred earlier, is giving us back a language of interconnectedness, belonging and wholism. Without going into detail, whereas the science of modernity was dominated by analysis, by breaking things down into their component parts, by starting from the bottom up in trying to make sense of the world, the physicists and meteorologists who have contributed to chaos theory have begun somewhere else. Many phenomena, not least weather clouds, are best explored in the contexts of whole systems, of the ways in which everything affects everything else, rather than in discrete analysable units. The language of systems, of networks, of connection is much more common in the science text books of this generation than it was a generation ago.

Perhaps new discoveries in physical science are reminding us again of what the theologians of centuries ago knew in a much less sophisticated way: that all things hold together. As St Paul puts it, 'in him all things hold together' (Colossians 1.17). But then he immediately talks about the Church, the body of Christ in whom we are to grow, that corporate humanity which is the focus for the life of God's kingdom within this world.

There are many barriers in the way to our discovering, and to others discovering, how to grow up into Christ, how to love God and our neighbours and be just in human affairs. Some are sins, for which we all need to hear the word of forgiveness and grace. Some barriers are of ignorance – which is why we share the faith; some are of confusion and uncertainty – hence our search for truth; some are of loneliness, of pain, of being abandoned, of depression, of anxiety – we are called to serve our neighbour; some are of structures of injustice, of racism, famine, global inequities, ecological devastation – we must confront injustice.

And what is it all for? Seek first God's kingdom: that we may be real; that we may be like Christ; that we may help one another to grow nearer to Christ; that we – with all God's people here and world-wide, within the whole created order – may be caught up into the love of God the Holy Trinity. The redeeming love of Christ makes possible the renewal of the whole of God's creation. As Hans Küng put it: God's kingdom is creation healed.

Our fragmented and individualized Western society so badly needs to know that personal communion is possible. Our spiritually homesick culture needs to know that communion with the real God is possible. The Church does not often get it right. But if it is not happening in the Church, where will it happen? How are we to learn, together, gradually over time, with pain and struggle no doubt, to express in our relationship with God and with each other, and with all those we are called to serve, something of the grace of the Christ who loved us and gave himself for us? How (with apologies to Descartes!) are we to learn that 'we are loved – therefore we are'?

Chapter 6

WHOEVER BELIEVES

There are three themes to this chapter. First, we look briefly at the 'whoever' of our text and glance at the rich variety of religious experiences. Second, we explore the significance of 'belief' and what this might mean in a post-modern world. We will have in mind not only the way the era of modernity led to a narrow, instrumental, view of rationality, but also the way some post-modern thinkers have abandoned rationality altogether. The biblical understanding of faith-as-commitment opens the door to creative dialogue with those thinkers who are trying to recover a more fully rounded understanding of what it is to be 'rational'. Then third, we offer a short meditation on 'Encounter with the risen Jesus' as an exploration of what personal commitment might include.

Whoever

Several times we have commented on the fact that according to the Christian story, we are personal selves in all the mystery of being made as the divine image. When William James called his Gifford Lectures 'The Varieties of Religious Experience' (see Chapter 2 above), he was wanting to emphasize the fact that different people experience God in different ways. Since James's time there has been considerable development in personality psychology, and different factors used to describe our differences in temperament and style which affect the way we know God and relate to other people.

We turn back once again to the Fourth Gospel, which illustrates some of the very different responses Jesus shows to different people.

• Nicodemus, the half-believer, the academic, comes at night, and receives a fairly strong theological response calling him to nail his colours to the mast.

- The Samaritan woman at the well is treated very gently. Jesus puts her under an obligation by asking for a drink; he gently steers the conversation and waits for her response. He answers her questions at her own level, and eventually puts his finger on her conscience.
- The sick man at the pool of Bethesda is simply asked 'Do you want to be healed?'
- The man who had been blind from birth found Jesus touching his eyes and telling him to go and wash in the pool of Siloam. To his surprise he was made well, meanwhile Jesus had disappeared.
- With Martha and Mary at the grave of Lazarus there is reassurance, weeping, indignation and tenderness in Jesus' manner.
- Philip is told to believe; Peter is told to put up his sword.
- Pilate's arrogant question is turned back on him: You would have no power unless it had been given you.
- Mary Magdalene hears Jesus tenderly call her name.
- Thomas is invited to reach out and touch.
- Peter at the lakeside hears a word of forgiveness and reinstatement.

The Gospel explores Jesus' responses to half-believers and doubters, to the questioning and to the arrogant, from the joy of the village wedding to the grief at the village grave, from those who are hurting, or guilty, or blind, to those who need a word of reassurance, a word of rebuke, or a word of forgiveness. The characters in the story are all at different places in their own lives and journeys of faith. And in many of these stories there is mystery. Who was it that sinned that the man was born blind, him or his parents? Jesus does not answer the question but turns it round from the question about past causes to the future glory of God (John 9.2–3). The disciples marvel that Jesus is talking with a woman at the well but don't dare to ask him why. According to their own needs and in so many different ways, Jesus brings all these people nearer to the discovery that he is the Christ, the Son of God, and that in believing there is life in his name (cf. John 20.31).

Not only in the Gospels, but throughout Christian history there have been significant differences in people's responses of faith.[1] The Jewish believers in Jesus (Yeshua), in the middle of the first century, worshipped in the temple and sacrificed animals. They responded to the Hebrew Bible as their scriptures, held the seventh day as holy, and talked of Jesus as Messiah. The Greek believers a century or two later had other writings included in their scriptures, talked about Jesus as Lord, had nothing to do with the temple or sacrifice, and were very concerned with careful formulation of doctrines such as the Trinity which would have puzzled the first-century believers. At times, discipleship has been expressed by self-mutilation, by the discipline of standing in ice-cold water, by fasting for days on end in the desert. At other times by missionary zeal, Pentecostal exuberance, engagement in social and political activities. Some people have welcomed martyrdom as a sign of their faithfulness. Others have given their lives to the alleviation of suffering as a sign of theirs.

What creates all this variety is to some extent cultural preference, to some extent personal temperament, to some extent life experiences and the accident of birth. In their classic *The Social Psychology of Religion* (1975), Michael Argyle and Benjamin Beit-Hallahmi related the different ways in which people express their religious commitment to a range of social and cultural factors such as parental attitudes, educational influences, age, gender, socio-economic status and so on. To look at the ordered, dutiful mind of St Matthew, the breathless activity of St Mark, the questing journeyings of St Luke, the imagery and intimacy of St John, the endearing bluster of St Peter, the passionate theological mind of St Paul, to name but a few, is to see a range of religious responses from just a few of the authors of New Testament books. But what holds all this variety together within a shared Christian identity is shared belonging to the family of God made known in Jesus and expressed as the fellowship of his Holy Spirit. A Christian is someone baptized in the name of the Father and of the Son and of the Holy Spirit, and who therefore is committed to believing in Jesus Christ, and thereby finding life in his name.

The 'whoever' of our text is a sign of the divine welcome to all without discrimination or distinction. It is a reminder of the way the ministry of Jesus broke down barriers of exclusion to reach with the love of God towards those whom others believed did not belong. It must therefore rebuke all judgemental discrimination between people and declare the love of God to all. Although the Sermon on the Mount (Matthew 5; 6; 7) does invite us to recognize clear boundaries between the worship of God and the worship of mammon, between the narrow way of obedience to God's word and the broad way of complacent abandonment of God's ways, it does also contain the stern rebuke against all man-centred judgemental condemnation: 'Judge not, that you be not judged.'

The common thread in this variety of experiences of encounter with Jesus is that of personal engagement and commitment. We see in him no detached observer, but one who is 'not untouched by the feeling of our infirmities' (Hebrews 4.15, Authorized Version), who in his incarnation assumes our frames of reference and comes where we are. We see in the variety of responses in those to whom Jesus spoke, engagement and personal response.

The invitation is to all: Repent, for the kingdom of heaven is at hand; Come to me all who are weary and heavy laden and I will give you rest; Follow me. It is based on the inclusiveness of God's love, who so loved the world that he gave his only Son that *whoever* believes in him should not perish but have eternal life.

Believes

What does it mean to believe? Unfortunately, belief has too often been reduced to the idea of assent to certain propositions, in the sense that the White Queen believed six impossible things before breakfast. But to reduce belief to propositional assent is the high road to some of the fundamentalisms which so bedevil Christianity and some of the other credal world faiths.

Of course there is an essential credal component to Christianity. In some of what we have already said about Jesus Christ, and about the various signals of transcendence we have noted, the claim is implicit that these give us glimpses of God because they are caught up into a 'big story' about God's purposes for the world, a story told in the life of Israel recorded in the Old Testament, in the life and teaching of Jesus Christ borne witness to in the New Testament, a story constantly re-enacted in the liturgies and life of the Christian Church throughout the centuries and throughout the world. In other words, it is a story that understands itself both as a witness to and a response to God's self-revelation. Christianity is a credal religion. But to regard revelation as merely something proposi-tional would be like treating a solid object as though it were merely two-dimensional. Credal words and propositional state-ments are themselves only signals, pointers beyond, to the more-than-personal Reality who is God.

To believe, in the sense in which the Fourth Gospel uses the phrase, is another whole dimension to faith than assent to credal statements. In fact the noun *pistis* is hardly used in the Johannine literature. Rather we find the verb *pisteuo* – to believe, and frequently that comes in the phrase, as in our key text, *pisteuo eis* literally translated 'believe into'. In his comment on St John's usage, R. K. Lee writes: 'The orthodox creed is not a victorious power except it is received by faith; still less has the act of faith any moral significance apart from its object' (Lee, 1962, p. 229). Further, there is also a sense in the Fourth Gospel that faith is not simply an attainment, it is a process of constant growth. Thus John 20.31 includes the word *pisteuete* which has the sense: 'that you may *grow in the belief that* Jesus is the Christ, the Son of God'. Jesus' words to Thomas also suggest that believing is a process which goes on con-tinually (John 20.27). When St John speaks of believing, therefore, he is talking not about assent, but about commit-ment, engagement, participation, growing personal trust.

Participation and commitment

By contrast, much of the style of Enlightenment thought was

not of commitment, but of detachment, not of participation but of disengagement. The positive side to this was the growth of a science which sought to be as objective as possible in its quest for the truth, and of methods of analysis which have gradually uncovered the basic building blocks of the universe. Science was thought of mostly in terms of gathering together positive information provided through an analysis of sense data. It became the positivist programme which then assumed that all knowledge was of this sort, and that the task of science was to collect facts into bundles. So 'facts' became separated from personal 'values'; science became the route to all true knowledge; anything supernatural was consigned to the sceptic's bonfire. Enlightened human reason ruled the world.

As we have tried to show in Chapter 3, there is a great deal about science – in the sense of seeking the truth about God's world – for which we thank God, and whose benefits we daily enjoy. Nothing in this chapter is meant to detract from the massive benefits to all humanity which modern science has brought. However, the two fellow-travellers technology and 'instrumental reason' are both much more ambiguous.

Through the developments of modernity, science, the quest for truth – 'thinking God's thoughts after him' – became superseded by the gradual fusion of science and technology, with a commitment to the priority of technique, and the growth of a technological mind-set which believed that by asking the right questions, and by technical intervention, human beings inevitably would find the right answers, and improve their world. This is part of what is meant by 'instrumental reason'. Industrialization, concentration on production, and urbanization, are the result of the growth of technology. Although there has been enormous benefit to humanity through this achievement, we are now also taking stock of the environmental costs of some industrial progress. Pollution and nuclear weapons are but two results of a technology which, though a good servant, can be a destructive master.

Some of the anxieties about technology – the uses to which pure science is put, and for which, as I say, there is much to thank God – were well expressed some years ago by Walter Thorson, who even speaks of 'the end of the age of science'. In the considerable fusion of the physical sciences with technology, it is the philosophical much more than the physical impact which is important:

> Having finally understood that scientific truth is a source of power, man has made the crucial decision that from now on the will to power and the uses of power should dictate the relevance and value of that truth ... The fusion of science and technology means that, increasingly, the moral decisions as to the uses of truth will be made pre-emptively before the truth is even sought; we shall seek only truth which fits our purposes. (Thorson, 1978, pp. 217f.)

What Thorson means is that factors such as the economic pressure from government and from industry, in the allocation of research grants and so on, will so dictate the priorities of science that we will effectively end up with a 'cost-benefit manipulation of truth'.

The broadening again of rationality
If a major component of modernity is the narrowing of reason to only what we have called instrumental reason, the responses of post-modernity have been both positive and negative. Inevitably for some the reaction is of the abandonment of reason altogether: ultimately of despair and meaninglessness. The whole basis of the Enlightenment project is rejected, leading for some writers to a realization of Nietzsche's nihilistic vision of a world in which not only God is dead. In this respect, Nietzsche was an early post-modern thinker.

However, other commentators on modernity, such as Jürgen Habermas, are trying to hold on to the positive values of the Enlightenment, and so return to a more broad, practical and positive view of human reason. In briefest summary, Habermas wants to put the Enlightenment project back on course again. He rejects the narrowing of reason down to simply instrumental technique, and develops a view of reason which recovers the sense that human beings are conscious agents in the processes of knowing, and are engaged in knowing through language and action.[2] He speaks of three 'cognitive interests': what he calls the *technical*, by which he means the form of the analytical-empirical sciences; the *practical*, by which he means the use of historical and hermeneutical disciplines to provide an understanding of meaning; and crucially the *emancipatory*, by which he means the basic quest for non-distorted communication between people concerning what is known, and the fact that this knowledge is personally empowering, liberating and creates responsibility. Knowledge, in other words, is essentially to do with *personal communicative action*.

Knowledge through participation
Another philosopher trying to rescue a broader understanding of rationality from positivism is Michael Polanyi. It was he who brought the word 'commitment' back into the philosophy of science (cf. Polanyi, 1958; 1966; 1969). As we noted in Chapter 3, Polanyi argues that there is no such thing as a wholly objective detached science.[3] All knowledge includes an inescapably personal commitment. Science, indeed, we ventured to suggest, is itself a form of 'faith seeking understanding'. Even in the least personal of the sciences, physics, the processes of discovery, the formulation of theories, the procedures for testing hypotheses all involve a personal commitment on the part of the scientist. Evaluation of results, for example, is often a matter of statistical correlation and of weighing probabilities. But these are not scientific concepts – they involve personal judgement based on experience and skill. Equally, the use of apparatus, the way results are recorded, even the choices of the topic of research in the first place, involve personal evaluations based on a commitment to the subject matter under investigation. Discovery is rooted in the conviction that there is something there to be found, and that our theory will then open up knowledge of hitherto undreamed-of possibilities.

True knowledge, Polanyi argues, arises through participation, or, as he says, 'indwelling'. To give one example: I cannot tell you how to ride a bicycle. It would be possible to assent to all the mechanics involved in cycle riding without knowing how to ride. I know how only through doing, through participating. My feet 'indwell' the pedals, which thus become an extension of myself for the purpose of riding. I am, however, only tacitly aware of the pedals. In fact, if I concentrate on the pedals, I will fall off. But I use this tacit knowledge as part of my total knowledge of bicycle riding which is a knowledge attained not by detachment, but by participation, by commitment. The knowledge arrived at by scientific discovery is also, according to Polanyi, a knowledge by participation. His whole approach to the philosophy of science goes against the Enlightenment paradigm of knowledge by detachment.

Christian thinkers should well understand what Polanyi means by indwelling, participation, commitment. We are not gods, standing over the world with our superior detached rationality. We are both part of the world, indwelling it, and also able to transcend it through our God-given powers of perception, imagination and reason. We know through taking part. This is very close to the 'belief into' of which the Gospel of John speaks. The invitation is for 'whoever' to know through taking part, through commitment, through participation in the life of Christ, through believing into him.

Another word to describe an appropriate personal response such as this is 'responsibility'. The true nature of personal responsibility is the appropriate personal response to the situation in which we find ourselves (cf. Niebuhr, 1963). One of the features of Jesus' ministry is that he creates in people the capacity for exercising responsibility. Part of becoming more fully alive is exercising appropriate responsibility for ourselves and our world – and that begins in an appropriate response to the God who invites our participation and commitment.

But commitment to anything or to anyone is not something that comes easily, or indeed makes much sense, in a culture which has forgotten how to develop the capacity to make commitments. For Christian mission to encourage the 'whoever' to 'believe in him', requires the Church also to take very seriously the need to create environments in which we can all be helped to grow the sort of characters which are capable of making commitments. In other words, be helped to take responsibility for our choices, our lives, the world we are in.

Encounter with the risen Jesus

We can bring together some of the threads of our earlier discussion with a biblical meditation on a particular religious experience – namely that of the two disciples on the road to Emmaus described in Luke chapter 24.

'Yes, it is true. The Lord has risen!' That was the response of the disciples in Jerusalem when Cleopas and his companion returned from Emmaus. What does it mean to say something is true? How do we know whether something is true? There are people who understand 'truth' to be something to do with ideas, beliefs, ideals. Truth is something in the mind – and that may or may not correspond with reality.

Cleopas said at one point to the stranger who joined them on the Emmaus road, 'Our hope had been that Jesus would be the one to set Israel free.' There was a whole set of assumptions, hopes, ideas about God doing the rounds in Jerusalem. God's new age would dawn. God's kingdom would be established. God's Messiah would liberate his people from Roman rule. And now Jesus had come. Now must be the time for God's intervention in the political system. The truth about God was focused for these people in the hope of political liberation.

But a lot of it was a truth they had concocted in their own heads. If we push this sort of approach towards its extreme we could call it idealism. This is truth constructed from my hopes, my ideas, my needs, the way I construe the world. And of course there is a sense in which all this is part of the story.

But idealism is not enough. As the disciples on the road to Emmaus illustrate, it needs to be tested against the hard realities of the physical world. Their hoped-for Messiah had been executed. Jesus had been crucified. Their view of truth had given way to disappointment and disillusionment. This was not the way God was supposed to work. God's king should not suffer. God had not fitted the picture they had of him. God had not come up to their expectations. Their idealized truth ran aground on the hard rocks of suffering.

There are other people who understand truth to be something essentially physical. Some might call this scientific truth – truth which comes to us through our senses, truth in what we can weigh and measure and put in a bottle. Truth for such people is not about ideas but empirical facts which are testable.

And here the other side of Cleopas illustrates what I mean. The brute fact was that Jesus was dead. The empirical data were inescapable. Therefore there could be no further hope. Therefore the women who had claimed to see the tomb empty could not be trusted. Perhaps after all the only truth is the evidence of our own eyes.

And if we push this approach towards its extreme we would could call it positivism. And there are plenty of positivists around today, such as those among the scientists whose view is that truth only comes through the data of our senses, and that everything is ultimately explainable in terms of physics and chemistry. They have no room for any concept of God – other than religion being a sort of universal virus which we might catch if we are not careful; no room for any idea that a crucified Messiah might rise from the dead.

But positivism is not enough either. It will not do to say that all life, and love and beauty and faith, purpose, suffering and tragedy, are simply the movement of molecules in the brain. We have criticized such reductionism before. Ordinary human life itself points beyond the merely physical.

The centre of this passage about the road to Emmaus is that there is an approach to truth beyond idealism and beyond positivism. Cleopas has to learn to see what happened to Jesus not only in terms of political hopes, nor only in terms of physical crucifixion. The stranger on the road explained this to Cleopas: 'O foolish men, and slow of heart to believe all that the prophets have spoken! Was it not necessary that the Christ should suffer these things and enter into his glory?' Your categories are too small. Your idealism does not have room for what your own prophets told you: this is a Christ who does suffer. Your idealism is not big enough to deal with the physical realities of a suffering world. But then your depressed positivism is not big enough either. By seeing only Jesus' physical death, you do not have room for God's purpose, you do not have room for the suffering Christ also entering into glory, you do not have room for resurrection.

The experience in the present on the road to Emmaus is of a stranger expounding to them in the scriptures the things concerning himself. And the stranger is accepting their offer of hospitality, and breaking bread with them. He has been with them unknown, in all their explorings. He has been the truth for them, even in their unknowing. Jesus Christ makes himself known through personal encounter.

Then their eyes were opened and they recognized him. Then they realized why their hearts had been burning within them on the road.

So here is a deeper, experiential way of understanding truth: truth as encounter.[4] Truth in the paradox of a God who suffers with us. Truth in the mystery of a crucified man who now lives among us. Truth in the encounter of the present moment as disciples meet the risen Christ who expounds the scriptures which make their hearts burn, and breaks the bread which opens their eyes. Truth as they commit themselves then to act on what they believe.

The Emmaus story points us to a God who suffers with his world – the truth of a God who encounters us in the middle of our questions and our struggles; a God who not only enters this world's suffering but transforms it, who gives hope to the hopeless, and life to the dead. This is a faith to live by and a faith to die by. Resurrection is not part of the usual physical processes of nature. Resurrection speaks not of a closed system but of a world open to God's recreative love and power. Resurrection speaks of a God who makes things new.

And this experience of God is discovered on the road to Emmaus in the moment of encounter. But it could be on the Old Kent Road, or Tottenham Court Road, or the road to Mandalay. If it is true that the Lord has risen, he is a Lord who comes alongside us, whether we recognize him or not, whichever road we travel. A God who reveals himself in a living encounter with the risen Jesus. That is a central theme in the mission of the Church.

The next chapter takes up in greater theological detail what such an encounter implies.

Chapter 7

SHOULD NOT PERISH, BUT HAVE ETERNAL LIFE

This last phrase of our key text opens up a huge theological territory about death and life, judgement and mercy, earth and hell and heaven. We cannot unpack all of this now. But we can and must again note that this text comes in the middle of a discussion in the narrative of John's Gospel between Jesus and Nicodemus. It is about being born anew and seeing the kingdom of God. It is about the life-giving Spirit of God who blows where he wills. It is especially related to the health-giving lifting up by Moses of a brass serpent on a pole in the desert – with a reminder that all the people afflicted with diseases who looked up found health again. This serves as an analogy to the cross on which Jesus Christ was lifted up.

It is about the exposure of evil by the light of God. It is essentially about death and resurrection. So when John 3.16 speaks of 'believing into' Jesus Christ, and that those who do so believe should not perish but have eternal life, we are to understand this in relation to the death and resurrection of Jesus, and to the believer being united in some way with Jesus in his death and in his resurrection life.

One of the questions this text poses for us, therefore, is: 'How does the story of Jesus, and especially of his death and resurrection, impinge on our human stories – on my story?'[1]

In Chapter 5, above, we gave an outline of the way death and resurrection were part of Jesus' own story. We must now ask what this means for those who believe in him. Our text talks in terms of not perishing but having eternal life, and we will want to place these hopeful and purposeful phrases in the context of a culture of modernity which has tended to concentrate on human progress rather than divine purpose, and of post-modernity which very often seems to make a virtue of despair. Can the Church in its mission have reasonable grounds for continuing to preach a Gospel of hope?

Death and resurrection as part of our human stories

We begin with noting some of the characteristics of the 'old humanity' in which we all share. If we turn to Genesis 1–11 (cf. Atkinson, 1990), we find the stories there depicting an ambiguous human nature which at times enjoys God's blessing and at times is under God's curse. In the stories of Adam and Eve, Cain and Abel, Noah and Babel, the wonder of our humanity in the divine image is contrasted with stories of mistrust, shame, guilt and conflict. All relationships between people and God, people and each other, people and their environment, people within themselves, become estranged. Complementarity in the sexes becomes subordination; work becomes toil; mutuality and fellowship become banishment and alienation. This is the anatomy of disorder which can most broadly be described as the 'rule of death'. Instead of growth, creativity, freedom and fellowship, human life is instead, or as well, marked by the anxiety of mistrust, the frustration of shame, the bondage of guilt and the loneliness and bitterness of conflict.

It is fascinating how Erik Erikson's psychosocial approach to human development picks up on many of these themes. In 'The eight ages of man' (1951, ch. 7), he suggests that these processes usually include critical phases in which the growing person has to deal with various tensions in their personal and interpersonal lives. The most basic question for the baby is whether the external world is ultimately trustworthy or not. As the baby grows, will his life be marked by autonomy or shame, by initiative or guilt, by industry or inferiority? Will the adolescent's life be noted for a sense of identity or one of confusion; will a person be able to offer intimacy in relationships, or will she be isolated in loneliness? Will adult life be one of creativity and integrity, or of stagnation and despair?

Erikson holds out the hope that in good human maturing, the positive aspects of each critical phase will outweigh the negative. Yet we all know that there is in human nature the struggle which he describes in terms of mistrust, shame, guilt, inferiority, confusion, isolation, stagnation and despair. Here is a developmental psychologist describing what we might call the 'rule of death'.

When Peter Berger described his 'signals of transcendence', one example that he gave is of the universal human hope that death is not the end.

> It is precisely in the face of the death of others, and especially of others that we love, that our rejection of death asserts itself most loudly. It is here, above all, that everything we are calls out for a hope that will refute the empirical facts ... a No! to death is profoundly rooted in the very being of man. (Berger, 1969, p. 83)

That No! is surely also the motivation for Dylan Thomas's angry poem in the face of the death of his father:

> Do not go gentle into that good night.
> Rage, rage against the dying of the light.

The sense of disorder is also powerfully explored in Shakespeare's *King Lear*:

> These late eclipses of the sun and moon portend no good to us. Though the wisdom of nature can reason it thus and thus, yet nature finds itself scourg'd by the sequent effects: love cools, friendship falls off, brothers divide; in cities, mutinies; in countries, discord; in palaces, treason; and the bond crack'd twixt son and father ... We have seen the best of our time: machinations, hollowness, treachery, and all ruinous disorders, follow us disquietly to our graves. (I.2)

Psychologist, sociologist and poet are all profoundly disturbed by the negative, disordered, destructive dimensions of the 'rule of death' in life, and yet hold out a hope that life must be more than this.

It is at this point that Leon Morris's book *The Cross of Jesus* (1989) rings true. He argues that the atonement is vaster and deeper than many of the traditional theories suggest. He presents the Cross as God's response to the human experience of futility, ignorance, loneliness, sickness, selfishness and death. This seems to me to provide a language of atonement for today. Whereas some patristic authors understood the cross mostly in terms of slavery and ransom; whereas Anselm opens us to the feudal categories in which sin is understood as dishonour, and Calvin uses his legal mind to focus mostly on guilt and acquittal; whereas in 1930s Europe, Aulén's *Christus Victor* could catch the headlines with its return to the military categories of conquest, today we need to hear more about sin in the terms we drew from the Genesis prologue: mistrust and alienation, shame, guilt, conflict and disorder.

By *mistrust*, I mean anxiety and frustration in the face of an uncertain world, in which powers greater than our own threaten us. By *shame*, I mean our own sense of personal failure, and the inability to hold up our heads with confidence and gratitude that we are who we are. By *guilt*, I mean the state we put ourselves in through violation of God's moral character. By *conflict*, I mean the confusion, alienation and isolation in our relationships with one another and with our environment.

One of the key features of Jesus' life is his identification with the poor, the outcast, those who are under threat. In Nazareth he applies to himself the prophecy in Isaiah concerning good news for the poor, release for the captives, recovery of sight to the blind and the setting at liberty those who are oppressed. He is known to be on the side of the outcasts and sinners, and eating with them (e.g. Luke 15.2).

This process is seen at its fullest in Jesus' own taking on himself the rule of death, and yet being raised to life again. In the Gospel narrative of the Passion, trial and crucifixion of Jesus, we see a man betrayed – his whole environment was untrustworthy. Even his closest friends forsook him and fled. We see a man naked and exposed to mockery and shame. We see a man dying alone. We see the agony of uncertainty in the Garden, and the agony of separation from the fellowship of his Father in the cry of dereliction: 'My God, my God, why have you forsaken me?' St Paul reminds us that such a death is the death of one who is cursed by God (Galations 3.13; cf. Deuteronomy 21.23). He sums up the whole experience for us in the remarkable phrase that God 'made him to be sin, who knew no sin' (2 Corinthians 5.21). Jesus experienced in his passion, trial, suffering and crucifixion all the effects of the rule of death in human life.

> A sight most pitiful in the meanest wretch,
> Past speaking of in a king! (*King Lear*, IV.6)

And then in Jesus' resurrection, we see what we might call the death of the rule of death. As Calvin put it Jesus 'let himself be swallowed by death, as it were, not to be engulfed in its abyss, but rather to engulf it' (Calvin, 1536, II.16.7).

The New Testament describes Jesus' death as the means by which the rule of death in this world is broken. He, as it were, takes on death, dies its death, and yet is raised to new life. He partook of our nature, says Hebrews 2.14–15, 'that through death he might destroy him who has the power of death, that is, the devil, and deliver all those who through fear of death were subject to lifelong bondage'.

It is clear that we must speak of God's deliverance being made possible through the combined power of Jesus' death and resurrection. Without the resurrection, any talk of the power of Jesus' death is incomplete. The fourth-century theologian Athanasius speaks of the purpose of the Lord's dying, and of 'all dying in him', being 'that he might turn back to incorruption men who had reverted to corruption, and quicken them from death by the appropriation of his body and by the grace of his resurrection' (*De Incarnatione*, 8). Calvin makes a similar point, referring to Christ's death for our sins, and our being born anew to a living hope through the resurrection.

The hopeful language of being born is also taken up in Frances Young's book *Can These Dry Bones Live?*, in which she

explores Romans 8 and Paul's words about the redemption of
the whole creation which has been 'groaning in travail'. The
ambiguity, suffering and struggle of which the psychologists
and poets speak can also be understood as the labour pains of
God – to bring forth a new people, restoration, new life, new
hope. Professor Young links this to the strands of teaching
about hope in the New Testament. She concludes that such
teaching has two aspects:

> The first is its acceptance that the present state of the world
> is far from satisfactory. The second is confidence that never-
> theless it is all under God, and God's purposes will be
> worked out. Atonement is to do with making that hope
> credible. (Young, 1982, p. 54)

The Bible emphasizes that the motivation behind the death of
Jesus is the self-giving love of God, the God of life, whose
intusion of life into the rule of death opens up the possibility
that true human life can yet be lived. It is from the creative
heart of the Father that his saving love extends to his
disordered and perishing world. In our disordered and alienated world, one of us has broken through the power of this
world's disorders, and – like God in the opening of the creation
saga – has brought order again where there was chaos.

And now we can add that it is through the work of the Holy
Spirit, uniting us to the life and death of Jesus Christ, that the
Father's love, seen in Jesus, is shed abroad in our hearts,
bringing life where death rules. It is by reference to the work
of the Holy Spirit within the love of the Holy Trinity that we
can approach the question: what difference does the story of
Jesus make to my human story? What difference does the Cross
make to life? The answer of the New Testament is that we are
united with Christ in his death and in his resurrection.

The Cross and Resurrection do not affect us at all through
some legal fiction of imputed guilt and imputed righteousness
(as some have interpreted the penal substitution theory). The
Cross and Resurrection affect us because we are really and
truly united with the Christ who died and was raised. This is

the basis of Paul's argument in Romans 6.5: 'If we have been united with him in a death like his, we shall certainly be united with him in a resurrection like his.'

Forgiveness

The traditional categories of atonement theology are sin and forgiveness. I have tried to broaden the concept of sin to include not only the moral guilt of ungodly behaviour, which separates us from fellowship with God, but the wider themes of mistrust, shame, guilt and conflict.

Forgiveness, likewise, can have a narrower or a broader focus. I suggest that forgiveness is essentially a relational word. Forgiveness is appropriate in a situation where things are wrong. It does not pretend that there is no wrong. It does not offer peace at any price. Forgiveness is a dynamic process of change. Forgiveness breaks down the idealizations that pretend the world is all angel or all devil; it recognizes ambiguity: that there is real evil, wrong, and injustice, but that there is also hope of change. Forgiveness attempts to respond to wrong in a way that is open to new possibilities, seeking to reshape the future in the light of what is wrong in the most creative way possible. Forgiveness moves beyond the determinisms of fatalistic anxiety, despair of change, the law of retaliation, the bitterness of resentful conflict. Forgiveness is costly, and hard work, but essentially filled with hope. In other words, forgiveness is the process by which the life of resurrection, through the power of the Holy Spirit, engulfs, transforms and replaces in us the rule of sin and death. Forgiveness is a process, a journey, a pilgrimage – even an adventure. Forgiveness is a relationship word, and as with all relationships, it happens over time, not all at once.

Let us see what forgiveness means in response to four of the features of what we earlier called the rule of death.[2]

Mistrust
What difference does the Cross and Resurrection of Jesus make to someone who is given up to anxiety? For some people,

anxiety is terrifying. The world is filled with terrifying powers over which I have no control. I may be stuck in what Ezriel called a 'required relationship' – a pattern of life and attitude from which I dare not move, because if I were to move there would be some terrible catastrophe, a hole would open in the universe and I would fall down it. Some of us hold on to depression, because what underlies the depression is too awful to face. For others, the feelings may not be so debilitating, but are none the less their basic attitude to the world. The world is not safe.

So I build idols to worship, to take my mind off life's uncertainties. Humankind, as T. S. Eliot (1974, p. 190) said, cannot bear very much reality. I put my faith in horoscopes, tarot cards, the stars, materialism, noise, other people who will come and rescue me; perhaps parents deify their children. Wayne Oates quotes Paul Tillich: 'Idolatry is the elevation of a preliminary concern to ultimacy.' When our devotion is given to something partial, conditioned, finite, we are resting our faith on something very fragile, and transient. 'Gordon Allport identified one characteristic of the mature religious sentiment as being comprehensiveness. To fix one's life commitment on a restricted, finite and temporary object of devotion is to have a non-comprehensive sentiment in one's faith' (Oates, 1973, p. 204). But it is sometimes easier, at least temporarily, to give in to the unreality of the images of 'the real world' which press upon us from the culture around, and then we despair that we cannot live up to these unreal expectations. We live in untruth, not in faith, trust and obedience.

By contrast, forgiveness opens up the possibilities of hope, again. In his Cross and Resurrection, Jesus Christ has gone the way of anxiety and despair before us. He is the pioneer who, for the joy that was set before him, endured the cross, despising the shame. He has gone the way of uncertainty, ahead of us, and broken the powers that so frighten us. The ineffectiveness of these other gods is now shown up.

Repentance of the sin of idolatry means to change one's god from a constricted, narrowed and dying god to a universal, comprehensive and eternal God. This calls for a change of mind, a transformation of loyalty, and a release of one's clutch on family, nation, denomination, race, sex, school, teacher, or ideological bias ... (Oates, 1973, p. 205)

And if God did not spare his own Son, will he not with him also freely give us all things? Nothing in the whole of creation can now separate us from his love (Romans 8.31–9). Our hope now lies in the fact that he promises to hold on to us in our uncertainties. Through the valley of every shadow he is with me.

God himself suffers there where the Crucified hangs. That is what all this means. When he cries 'My God, my God, why hast thou forsaken me?' the eternal Heart abandons itself to all the forsakenness and despair that a man suffers in his separation from God. Nothing more stands between God and me, because he has become my brother. At the bottom of every abyss he stands beside me. (Thielicke, 1969, p. 117)

I can therefore cast my care onto him, for by his death and resurrection he has brought me, really and truly, into the place where I know that he cares for me, and that all things will one day be brought to their fulfilment in him (cf. Ephesians 1.7–10). If sin is about mistrust, idolatry and lack of faith, forgiveness through the death and resurrection of Christ is about God's providence, about what Oates calls 'the enlargement of life', about coming more fully alive. This is a journey of pilgrimage, a living in hope. The evil powers have been conquered. As St John put it, 'We know that the Son of God has come ... Little children, keep yourselves from idols' (John 5.20f.).

Shame

What difference does the Cross and Resurrection of Jesus make to someone who is shrivelled through shame? Shame, says Bonhoeffer, only comes into existence in a world of division (Bonhoeffer, 1959). He is talking about the division between man and woman, and how in the Garden they were naked and not ashamed. But the division between them means that neither can now lift up their heads with confidence before the other. Shame also expresses the division within myself – between my hopes, desires and aspirations, and my failure, falling short and disappointment. Through my own wrong-doing as well as through my failure to achieve, I believe myself to be of little worth. My self-esteem is low. I do not like myself. And I am wading, head turned down, in a murky pool of stagnant water – the water of my disappointed hopes, lost opportunities, inability to reach the standards I and others had set. If my personal worth depends on my achievements, I am not worth much.

Sometimes the patterns of attitude and behaviour are associated with habits which I would prefer to give up but cannot. It is at this point that some of the approaches to therapy and counselling (e.g. Glasser, 1965) are right to emphasize my personal responsibility for attitude change. Sometimes shame arises through an inappropriate self-aggrandizement to cover my sense of failure, which I then despise.

Forgiveness opens up the hope-filled resources of grace.

Forgiveness is rooted in the gift of God's grace to us in Christ. Through his death and resurrection, God loves us. We are given the gift of belonging to Christ, of knowing that he has held his head in shame, crowned with thorns, but now holds it high, crowned with glory. If we are incorporated into Christ in the whole story of his suffering and humiliation, as well as the power of his new life, our lives are set in a new place. The old equation, 'worth equals works', can now be replaced by 'worth is a gracious gift'. This, I think, is the existential meaning of the theological formulation, 'justification by grace through faith'. Jesus Christ is the Justified One, and I am justified by being incorporated into him.

When one comes to terms with, confesses, and rethinks his behaviour and makes a decision to change, a reward of forgiveness resides in the decision: He has now thrown off the sense of weakness and begun to feel real strength. The result of feeling genuinely forgiven is freedom from impotence and helplessness. The resolve itself is a source of strength. (Oates, 1973, p. 208)

And so forgiveness breaks down idealizations. I no longer have to think of myself in the either/or terms of wonderful and achieving, or failing and worthless. If I forgive myself, I realize that this side of heaven I will always to some extent get it wrong, I will fail, I will hurt people and they will hurt me. But I can also realize that my identity is not now defined by such things; my identity is centred – indeed given – elsewhere. I am now united with one who has identified with this world's failures and was not crushed by them. One who therefore is 'not untouched with the feeling of our infirmities', who can 'sympathize with our weaknesses' (Hebrews 4.15, AV and RSV) and who promises 'grace to help in time of need' (Hebrews 4.16).

If sin is about shame, forgiveness, especially of myself, is about the development of a realistic self-concept – to know myself as united with the crucified and risen Lord, with my identity now given, not through my own divisions and failure, but in grace. As Abelard says, the Cross manifests God's accepting love. Now I must put on love: 'If you then have been raised with Christ, seek the things that are above ... for you have died and your life is hid with Christ in God ... put to death, therefore what is earthly in you ... put on love' (Colossians 3).

Guilt

Part of the meaning of sin involves my moral accountability before God, as a person capable of choice. Whatever may be true of the limits within which my freedom is exercised, genetic or environmental, I still have the freedom to choose how much to collude with, confront, accept or deny the attitudes and patterns of behaviour with which I have grown up. I can understand my moral accountability in terms of a development from a prudential morality (in which I do certain things to avoid punishment or pain), through an authoritarian morality (in which I do certain things in response to external authority), to a personal morality (in which I take responsibility – within appropriate limits – for my choices and behaviour).[3]

To acknowledge my sin includes acknowledging that some at least of my choices and behaviour patterns are out of line with the purposes and character of God. Sin includes transgression, and its result is guilt. Guilt has both an objective dimension, as the state of a moral person who has violated or transgressed a moral law, and a subjective dimension, in which guilt is 'a feeling of having done something wrong, and cannot be analysed away into anything else' (McKeating, 1970, p. 16). This is that aspect of my personality commonly referred to as my conscience. (There is also what Buber calls 'civic guilt', the sort of legal guilt which arises through the infringement of certain social conventions – which may or may not include objective moral guilt. This does not concern us here.) I may be objectively guilty and not feel guilty (because my conscience has been worn down). I may subjectively feel guilty when I am not objectively guilty (because my conscience is over-scrupulous).

If I am to speak of sin in relation to guilt, I am referring primarily to the objective moral state of having violated God's purposes, law and character. It is a refusal, as Barth says, to let God be God. This may or may not include some subjective feelings associated with this. But true moral guilt is a trap, a bondage, from which I need to be set free. Behind wrong behaviour usually also lies a false belief. Behaviours are the expression of faith, which is why Paul says, 'Whatever does not proceed from faith is sin' (Romans 14.23). The cognitive therapists, who work with the destructiveness of irrational beliefs and their consequent behavioural responses, remind us of the trap of guilt which follows wrong faith and wrong doing. By contrast, forgiveness liberates me from condemnation, and enables me to live in freedom. It can speak of the truth which sets free. How does this happen?

The Object Relations approach of Melanie Klein is the nearest I think psychological theory gets to providing a model of the inner changes which forgiveness brings. Klein illustrates the emotions of our adult world by reference to what she calls their 'roots in infancy' (Klein, 1975). In Klein's understanding, the maturing process in the child goes through various stages. For a child who has related to mother in contradictory ways (the nourishing mother whom I love; the depriving mother who leaves me to cry, whom I hate), the development to seeing the mother as a whole person – sometimes nourishing, sometimes depriving, includes a realization of true guilt, namely that I have screamed at the one who is my provider and who loves me. There is a deep sense that wrong must be punished and a penalty paid. How is the child to move from incapacitating guilt to the capacity to give and receive love creatively towards mother and others? Klein says this comes through making reparation. Motherhood needs to provide the facilitating context in which emotional reparation can be made, and the demands of moral order satisfied. Then life can become creative.

Whatever we think of this as a model of child development (and the inner workings of a baby's mind are, of course, untestable), it provides a model for understanding the changes which forgiveness can bring in our adult world. For guilt to be handled, there must be reparation. The demands of right and wrong must be satisfied. Only then can life go on creatively.

In the Cross and Resurrection of Jesus, those strands of the New Testament which speak of the Cross in terms of God's curse, of an expression of divine wrath, and of the punishment for sin, are speaking of a divinely provided means by which reparation can be made. Anselm is right that God's honour needs to be satisfied, even if his model of satisfaction is inappropriate in a post-feudal world. Anselm is right that sin must be taken seriously. He is also right that only God can provide the means for making reparation. We must beware here of dividing up the Holy Trinity, as though the Son was appeasing the Father. I would suggest that one way of expressing this is to say that the interpersonal self-giving love within the persons of the Godhead flows out into the suffering and guilty world of persons who are trapped in their guilt, and in costly grace unites with them in their guilt, and then in them and on their behalf, makes the reparation needed to satisfy the honour of the God at whom we have screamed, despite his being our provider and the one who loves us. In Christ, God makes the costly reparation; in Christ, we are liberated to live creatively again.

This is close to the language of Romans, which pictures the consequences of sin in terms of four barriers between us and God: wrath, the condemnation of law, the power of sin, the rule of death. Paul's gospel is that through divinely provided and costly grace, we are 'free from wrath'; 'free from sin'; 'free from condemnation'; 'free from the law of sin and death' (Romans 5.9; 6.7; 8.1, 2).

Conflict

Part of the meaning of sin is conflict: this may be alienation between people and God or people and each other. It may be the destructive jealousy of Cain towards Abel, or the deep-seated vengeance of Lamech. It may be the disintegration of society as a whole, through its abandonment of a centre in God (as at Babel). It may show itself in the way we take our stand on the law of retaliation: you owe, so you must pay – a law which Jesus repudiates in the parable of the unjust steward. It is perhaps most evident in the third of what Stephen Neill calls the 'three great enemies of the human race: fear, frustration and resentment' (Neill, 1959, ch. 8). Resentment is a bitterness which cripples, decays, destroys.

Many of the other aspects of sin are included in this destructive kaleidoscope of conflict. As Oates puts it:

Sin as alienation from God and man is the composite and end result meaning of sin. Idolatry alienates one from God and those persons and/or things that are put in God's place. Shrinking back from participating with God and man in the demands of growth in personal and corporate life alienates and estranges a person. Destructive habits preoccupy and hinder one's relationships to self, others and God. Dividing walls of hostility estrange the self-elevated and ambition-ridden person. The foolish person seems to be asking to be cast out, estranged and isolated. (Oates, 1973, p. 211)

And the result is enmity not only between us and God, but between people, between cultures, between races, between ourselves and our environment. We stand on our rights, we demand our dues, we insist on fairness, we trample on one another to get it.

Forgiveness, by contrast, is a refusal to be trapped by the law of retaliation. Forgiveness is a willingness to move beyond the requirements of mere fairness into the justice which reflects the redemptive justice of God. Forgiveness does not demand an eye or a tooth, but is willing – in costly sacrifice – and without minimizing wrong, to seek to make good the wrong as far as possible, and move from stultifying bitterness and resentment into the fresh air of grace.

In the Cross and Resurrection, God does not demand his dues from us. In costly self-giving he vindicates his justice and righteousness from within his own heart. But he moves beyond requirement into gift; beyond death into life. Forgiveness is about life continuing despite the rule of death.

There are personal, social and political dimensions to forgiveness. *Personal* forgiveness may be seen in conflict-resolution between marriage partners; in the recognition of and repentance from blame-shifting, domination, manipulation of one person by another; it may be seen in the healing of memories in a person who has been hurt or abused; the letting go of a justified sense of bitterness in one who has been unjustly treated by another. It is seen in the grace spoken of by Peter:

To this you have been called, because Christ also suffered for you, leaving you an example, that you should follow in his steps. He committed no sin; no guile was found on his lips. When he was reviled, he did not revile in return; when he suffered, he did not threaten; but he trusted to him who judges justly. He himself bore our sins in his body on the tree, that we might die to sin and live to righteousness. By his wounds you have been healed. (1 Peter 2.21–4)

Social forgiveness would provide a creative contrast to the ingrained habits of our culture which seem to insist and require that people's sins accumulate against them. A politician who falls into sin may come to repentance, may start a new life, and may give himself into the service of others. Before God his conscience may now be clean, and the past put behind him. Not so with the tabloids who keep his story alive, the film-makers who set the story in celluloid, those who will always associate his name with his faults, and will not let him be free.

Can there be a *politics* of forgiveness?[4] Does not the biblical concept of justice indicate the appropriateness of certain political responses to evil in the world which are very close to what in personal terms we would call forgiveness? Such an approach would refuse to be trapped in a fatalistic determinism. It would refuse peace at any price but seek to vindicate justice in the face of wrong. It would not stop at settling scores, but would seek to move beyond conflict into a fresh creative political situation for the future. The history of the ending of apartheid, and the work of the Truth and Reconciliation Commission in South Africa, give some pointers to what a politics of forgiveness might involve.

Forgiveness seeks to approach the wrongdoer not in terms of bare retaliation and retributive justice alone, but in a way that is creative of new possibilities. It underlines the reality of human frailty and sin, and the limited capacity of human resources to deal with them, but for the sake of the common good it seeks to explore ways of handling wrong and guilt creatively and not destructively. Forgiveness involves a gracious initiative from the party who is wronged. Without forgiveness in the political arena, the options open seem to be either to reject the notion that politics is about conciliation and about making the best of faulty people, limited resources and a distorting heritage, or to abandon all quest for justice in human affairs and to acquiesce in injustice. Can a state's response to evil be both just and redemptive?

The most poignant biblical example of the difficulties and possibilities of conflict resolution at personal, social and political level is the relationship in the early Church between

Jew and gentile. That there was discord is evident from
Galatians and from the Acts. Attitudes of mutual condemnation in gentile and Jew are clear in the early chapters of
Romans. But Ephesians also speaks of those who were far off
being brought near in the blood of Christ.

> For he is our peace, who has made us both one, and
> has broken down the dividing wall of hostility ... that he
> might ... reconcile us both to God in one body through the
> cross, thereby bringing the hostility to an end ... through
> him we both have access in one Spirit to the Father.
> (Ephesians 2.14–18)

In other words, through the death of Christ, and the gift of the
Spirit of the risen Christ, there is now one living body of Christ
in this world. Through our actual unity together in Christ, the
walls of hostility are breached. Galatians 2 says it even more
forcefully: because Christ has died, we, in him, have died to the
law (the understanding and application of which has acted as a
barrier between Jew and gentile). Therefore, whether I like it
or not, I am one with my neighbour. Within the body of
Christ, Jew and gentile, all are brothers and sisters 'for whom
Christ died' (Romans 14.15; 15.1–13).

Conclusion
In summary: forgiveness is part of the love which casts out fear;
part of the truth which sets free. Forgiveness extends beyond
the forgiveness of our sins in the narrow sense of our wrong
actions, to 'all other benefits of his passion',[5] within which I
would want to include all that makes for healing, wholeness,
shalom. Forgiveness is the secret of the atonement, namely that
there can be life through death.

> When thou dost ask me blessing, I'll kneel down, and ask of
> thee forgiveness: so we'll live, and pray, and sing, and tell old
> tales, and laugh at gilded butterflies. (*King Lear*, V.3)

Forgiveness is the relational part of the mystery of God's will which he set forth in Christ as a plan for the fullness of time, to unite all things in him (Ephesians 1.9f.). Forgiveness is the response of the gospel to people under the rule of death, given up to mistrust, shame, guilt and conflict. It is to them a gift of grace, an infusion of life into the rule of death. It is also a task: thereafter within the body of Christ, they are to put to death the old nature, and put on the new. This is a corporate as well as a personal journey, a process of change, as our stories are caught up into the on-going story of Christ in the purposes of God for his world. Beginning with Abraham, and through the story of Israel, focusing all God's judgement and mercy in Jesus Christ, especially his death and resurrection, catching us all up into him in the power of his Spirit, God is creating an authentically new humanity, the Israel of God, of which we are beginning to be part.

Simone Weill describes the grace which is God's response to the gravity of sin, in terms of 'the cross as a balance, as a lever. A going down, the condition of a rising up. Heaven coming down to earth raises earth to heaven' (Weil, 1952, p. 84).

The end of the story is the restoration of a renewed Israel, a renewed people of God, who are the true humanity of God's creative purposes. One day, in trust, openness, freedom and love, the nations gather round the throne of God's glory. Creation is healed. Humanity is fully alive. And the centre of their worship is a Lamb.

May the God of hope fill you with all joy and peace in believing, so that by the power of the Holy Spirit you may abound in hope. (Romans 15.13)

Chapter 8

TOWARDS A MISSIONARY THEOLOGY

The agenda for missionary theology arises out of a conversation between Christian faith and the practical needs of a changing world, in the context of trust in God the Holy Spirit, who is the Spirit of God's life in the world and in the Church. After a preliminary paragraph, this brief conclusion will draw together some of the threads of previous chapters, and propose an outline of priorities for mission in the contemporary world.

What kind of God? What kind of Church?[1]

How do we plan for the Church's mission in a way which maintains the priorities of the gospel? If we start with the Church, all too quickly the Church becomes viewed as but one human institution or organization among others, to be managed as efficiently as we arc able through the best available management techniques, governed by human decision making and human group dynamics. Of course institutional, management and group dynamics issues are important and unavoidable and, indeed, can be part of the way God works in the world, and part of the way we discover something of the truth of God and of ourselves in our interrelationships. Of course we need to exercise the most responsible stewardship over the assets and resources of the Church for which we are accountable – and we need to draw on the best available tools and understandings we can find in doing so. But the danger of starting with the Church is that this may well be all we think we are doing. And we shall have lost that essential dimension of

141

the nature of the Church – namely that it is a wonderful and sacred mystery, instituted by God for his purposes in the world, which through slavery and exodus, through exile and return, through death and resurrection, through persecution and victory always breaks out of purely human categories, and is always open to the renewing power and love of the Holy Spirit which carries an element of unpredictability, surprise and glory.

So what is God like? And what, therefore, should the Church be like? What is the message of the gospel for our culture?

The God we have been writing about is God the creator, and therefore initiator and sustainer of all life. The whole world is dependent on the Lord, the giver of life, and all human beings are made to be the image of God in the world. God's grace sustains all things. God's love is all-encompassing. God's purpose is to sum up all things in Christ. God, in other words, is alive and active apart from our ways of thinking of him or speaking of him, and apart from the institutional structures through which we seek to worship and serve him.

God, we have said, is revealed in the history of his covenant relationship with Israel and supremely in the life, teaching, death and resurrection of Jesus Christ, a revelation to which is borne authoritative witness in the scriptures of the Christian Church. God's action is expressed in generous, lavish, unde-served grace, a love for the whole created world. It is a love which flows from the vulnerability and pain of the cross and the victory of the resurrection. For God so loved the world that he gave his only Son that whoever believes in him should not perish but have eternal life. And then God strangely offers himself to the world not through schemes and careful institu-tional planning, but through vulnerable, earthen pots like us, through the struggle of suffering and crucifixion, through a prayerful pilgrim Church travelling light to many of the things of this world, but moving on in hope while often walking in the dark, through very ordinary people who are themselves recipients of undeserved grace, and whose lives are being shaped by the cross and resurrection of Jesus.

The first word of the gospel is that 'God so loved the world that he gave ...', and that God was incarnate in Christ 'reconciling the world to himself'. Its last word is about the kingdom of God's glory, which is also about the healing of all creation, and the fulfilment of all humanity in Christ. We have referred several times to Hans Küng's affirmation: 'God's kingdom is creation healed' (Küng, 1977, p. 231) and to Irenaeus' declaration: 'The glory of God is a human being fully alive'. At the centre is the ministry and mission of Jesus to save, to serve, to liberate. The gospel is not primarily about the Church. Jesus came to call people into the kingdom of God's glory; the Church is a means to that end.[2] This is the 'big story' which gives meaning to all our ordinary stories. Here is the source of meaning, of purpose, of hope.

But what kind of Church bears witness to that kind of God?

This is not the place for discussion of church structures or denominational allegiances, important though the one and problematic though the other may be. Nor is it the place for discussion of techniques for evangelism, patterns of ministry, or initiatives in renewal. We will content ourselves with a brief summary of the conclusions of our earlier chapters, and offer these as parameters for a missionary theology, the details of which need to be more closely worked out than I have either space or competence to do. They are set out in the final column of the table on page 145, which is developed from the earlier table on page 19.

Missionary theology and the tasks of the Church

My chemistry professor had said that, although it may be all very well for me, as a scientist he could not believe impossible things, among which he included the knowledge of God. Since he wrote to me I have heard from a humanist chaplain who offers himself as a 'celebrant for non-religious ceremonies, funerals, weddings, baby-namings and secular pastoral care'. In his letter to me he says that 'this life is the only one of which we have certain knowledge, thus implying a great responsibility for it'. I replied saying that I, too, placed a very high value on this life and on our 'great responsibility', but I took

Outline of themes

	Theology	Modernity	Post-modernity	Missionary theology
God …	theistic foundation	non-theistic foundations	incredulity to all metanarratives *or* recovery of transcendence	demonstrate reality of God (i) in worship (ii) through apologetics
so loved that he gave …	demonstrated love	subjective morality	moral relativism *or* recovery of Value	demonstrate love and justice in the world
his only Son …	persons-in-relation	loss of person	iron cage *or* recovery of wholism	create community
that whoever believes in him …	faith as commitment	priority of instrumental reason	denial of rationality *or* broadening of rationality	recover capacity for commitment and responsibility
should not perish, but have eternal life.	purpose and hope	belief in human progress; loss of purpose	embrace the void *or* recover sense of meaning and hope	demonstrate meaning and offer hope

issue with his use of the phrase 'certain knowledge', thinking that he meant what is popularly called scientific knowledge, and said I thought this needed to be unpacked.

'How can I know you?' I would like to ask him. I could operate at the level of analysis, put you on a slab, and find out what you are made of. I might end up with enough water to fill several bottles, enough carbon to make leads for a few pencils, enough iron to make a good sized nail, some calcium, potassium and so on. But would I know you the person? I think I would know – more or less certainly – quite a lot about what you are made of, but not know you.

But I know *you* at a different level. My knowing you depends on us both taking the risk of letting ourselves be known. It is more vulnerable and painful. It means venturing into personal communion – and that is something that, though it depends on our physics and our chemistry, cannot be reduced to them.

When Christians talk about knowing God, it is the latter personal knowledge, which involves vulnerability, risk and commitment, that they mean. I hope that if both the chemistry professor and the humanist celebrant were wanting to ask in a little more detail what it is that Christians mean when they bear witness to God, some of the themes of this book might be of interest. And if they were then to wonder where on earth some of these themes were being put into practice, I would like to think that a visit to a Christian church might illustrate them.

I hope, first, that they might find a church which *demonstrates the reality of God through its worship*.

We have noted the close link between mission and worship. That is partly to say that worship itself can be a vehicle for mission, and also that the activity of worship towards God, and of service for God in his world, are inseparably linked together. A form of worship which does not lead outwards into mission too quickly becomes self-absorbed, and religion becomes a personal hobby for those who like that sort of thing. Religion of this sort has been described earlier as 'extrinsic' – the sort of religion a person *uses*, perhaps for social acceptance, perhaps to bring them a sense of peace in their own lives. But it is different from 'intrinsic' religion – which a person *lives*, in which worship is integrally related to a person's whole character and lifestyle, and which necessarily shows itself in the outworking of the relationship with God in living for God in the world, with all its uncertainties, contradictions and ambiguities. True worship inspires and requires mission. The ancient story of the Tower of Babel shows how when God is removed from the centre of social life, and people start building up power-structures of their own, the result is social disintegration. The same thought was expressed by Archbishop William Temple in a phrase quoted by Kenneth Leech: 'The world can be saved from political chaos and collapse, by one thing only and that is worship.' Leech goes on to demonstrate that liturgy, which stretches our human capacity for awe and wonder, which catches up all our different religious experiences and offers them in praise, and which is in itself a social act, the offering of the whole community, itself partakes of mission. 'Our witness is rooted in the adoration of the one true God who demands total obedience and who undermines the powers of this world. The liturgy is the heart of the protest against the disorder of the world' (Leech, 1997, p. 185).

One of the most important tasks of the Church for the sake of the Kingdom is to set out the story of Christ, his death and resurrection, in such a way as to draw people towards the Kingdom, and that therefore underlines the importance of the quality of what is on offer in our church services. 'Unless we return to a liturgy that stirs the imagination of those who come primarily not to belong but to worship, we might as well close our [churches]' (Bomford, 1996, p. 22).

The meaning of mission will be evident as Christian believers demonstrate in prayer, in worship, and in their personal and corporate experience, that God is real.

I hope that my questioners might then discover that the church they have wandered into takes very seriously the task of making sense of the faith in the contemporary world. The task of what has usually been called apologetics – giving a reasoned *apologia* for the faith – goes back to the call of the First Letter of Peter to give 'a reason for the hope that is in you' (1 Peter 3.15, AV). As we have tried to illustrate, there are many ways in which the ordinarinesses of our human experience point beyond themselves to give glimpses of God. In a society dominated on the one hand by science and technology, and on the other by spiritualities of various sorts, occult books replacing religion on the shelves of High Street booksellers, and a wholesale ignorance of what the Church is for, let alone of the rich heritage of spirituality within its history and experience, there is a very high priority to be placed on making faith reasonable, and making reasoned faith known. One of the missionary tasks of the Church is to provide an environment in which true spirituality – what Jonathan Edwards called religious affections – can develop and grow.

True religion, said Jonathan Edwards, is known by its fruits. And the first fruit of the Spirit is love. For the Church to be caught up into the mission of God, it needs to be an environment of love, and in which love can grow. Our explorers in the faith will be helped if they discover that all the Christian talk about *love is demonstrated in practical service*. The love will be seen in personal character and moral vision, and the Church will be a school for character-building. The love will show itself in a commitment of care for others in the fellowship. It will overflow the boundaries of the Christian community, rebuking discrimination between peoples, into neighbour-love for all, including enemies. It will be dressed not in the robes of authority and power, but wrapped around in the lowly towel of the self-giving servant. It will find social and political expression at local community, national and global levels in the quest for justice, in responding to poverty and debt, in care for the environment, in concern for the future of the planet.

The Church will also be manifestly a covenant of care, a facilitating environment in which people can discover that they belong, and that in a world of alienation, fragmentation and loneliness, it is still possible to *create community*, share fellowship, be society, make relationships. This is one of the major tasks of the Christian community – to demonstrate in practice an alternative way of being, which answers to the aching longings so many lonely people have in a world which has forgotten what it is to be a neighbour.

I hope further that my enquirers might discover that the Church which sees itself as a school for character-building takes very seriously its educational work. I hope they will find the Church members helping one another learn again how to make and *sustain commitments*. The nurturing, educational and therapeutic tasks of the Church are as much part of its mission as anything else. They can assist us to have confidence in the faith, to make links between the faith and the ordinary business of muddling through, of living and working and loving in the world, to learn again to acknowledge that Jesus the servant is Lord of all things, of all space, of all time. They can help us learn how to mirror his servant/lordship in our corporate Church life. They can help us also learn how to find grace to take responsibility for ourselves, for each other, and for our world – to take very seriously, in other words, the demanding call to the discipleship of following Jesus Christ wherever he leads.

Religion is ultimately about meaning. It can be, and indeed often is, a drive for personal well-being, or for improving society. It can be understood as the strength for character-building and for creating healthier human relationships. It can be the source of values which hold communities together, the source of our creative imagination, the frame in which we interpret art or appreciate music. It can be our solace and peace at the time of death. But underneath and deeper than all these, religion is ultimately about meaning (cf. Polanyi and Prosch, 1975, esp. ch. 10). I hope our faith-explorers will discover that.

The Christian story, rooted in the history of Israel and centred in the life and death and resurrection of Jesus, is a story which for generations has held the meaning of the world. There are many other stories, myths, spiritualities which offer meanings of different sorts, and which are available in the supermarket of ideas. And then there are those in the post-modern world for whom 'meaning' has no meaning, and the end of whose road is not only the death of God, but the death of Value, the death of humanity. But the heart of the mission of the Christian Church is to live and indwell and tell and share the story that 'God so loved the world that he gave ...' It is a story which goes by way of beatings, sweat, tears and crucifixion to a life of vindication, healing and glory. This 'big story' of God's purposes for his world, beginning in his creative love, and leading to the kingdom of his glory, is a story which catches up into itself all the smaller stories of our lives, fears, joys and hopes and those of the communities within which we are set. To place our own stories within this larger context is both a reminder that we are all, this side of heaven, only ever on the way – and also an encouragement that all our stories find their meaning within the *ultimate purposes of God*. This does not solve all our questions. For now, much is only 'through a glass, darkly'. One day we shall see 'face to face'. But enough light comes through the glass to enable the shape of the story to be discerned, for substantial steps on the journey to be taken, and for us to be able to discover that God's grace will hold on to us despite all uncertainties.

This is a Story, I hope my questioners will discover, in which in the End, truth is demonstrable, value is real, justice is achievable, community can be rediscovered, reconciliations can be made, hope can be offered, meaning can be found, the whole of creation can be healed, and humanity can come fully alive.

Our missionary task is so to make it known, that 'whoever' will may hear, and may come to believe that Jesus is the Christ, the Son of God, and that believing may have life in his name.

NOTES

Introduction

1 There is a vast literature which it is beyond the scope of this book to review. Key texts include Bernstein, 1983; 1985; 1991; Derrida, 1978; various books by Michel Foucault, some summarized in Rabinow, 1984; Hart, 1989; Harvey, 1989; Lyotard, 1992; and Rorty, 1991. See also Taylor, 1989; and Habermas, 1987. A useful summary is found in Lyon, 1994. There have been some significant theological responses, among them: Thiselton, 1995; Allen, 1989; Lakeland, 1997; Reader, 1997; and Walker, 1996.

2 Originally from the Anglican Consultative Council.

3 In David Bosch's magisterial survey *Transforming Mission* (1992), he describes different models or 'paradigms of mission'. The Church has understood its mission in different ways at different times. In the New Testament, for example, Bosch describes mission as Matthew portrays it as making disciples; in Luke, as practising forgiveness and solidarity with the poor; in Paul, as an invitation to join the kingdom of the last days.

In grossly oversimplified summary, we can note the way Bosch describes the development of Christian mission during history of the Church.

In the first three centuries of the Church's life, there seems to have been a spontaneous style of church planting, coupled with the work of travelling healer/missionaries. Some of the better-known theologians of the early centuries (the Apologists) worked hard at demonstrating the credibility of the gospel by building bridges into the contemporary cultures, trying to find the very best in other faiths as a basis for Christian convictions to be shared. As Greek thought shaped the way the Church understood its life and mission, the Church became the bearer of the civilizing aspects of culture. The developments of the liturgy, of Christian art and of fine buildings became bearers of that culture. Mission became more church-centred.

In the medieval period, the Church took on more political responsibilities, and relations between church and state became increasingly close. Mission became identified at times with an extension of the ecclesiastical system. The Bishop of Rome was at the centre of world evangelization. Mission became understood to mean the mediation of truth and grace. At this time also, a different emphasis developed: the monastic communities were formed, and their special gift of building communities which could be agents of transformation in the world around them; priests and monks replaced healers and missionaries.

By the time of the Reformers in the sixteenth century and the Puritans in the seventeenth, the Church was understood by many less for mission than for fellowship. The focus tended to be much more on the individual Christian vocation than on the institutional life of the Church. There was a concern for godly living, and the growth of Christian character, as well as a desire to bring every aspect of life under the Lordship of Christ, so that individual Christians bore their witness in the secular and political world. By the nineteenth century, and the colonial period, there were overlapping concerns between imperialism and mission. People thought of the Western responsibility to civilize the rest of the world through the spread of the Christian gospel. The missionary movements often emphasized the cross of Christ and the lostness of 'the heathen'. There were political links between commerce and Christianity. The goal was set for world evangelization. Mission was sometimes inspired by revivalism, and sometimes this also led to social reform.

Chapter 1: Glimpses of God

1 Harries, 1993, p. 101. See also, for example, Gombrich, 1995; and 1979; Wolterstorff, 1980; Rookmaaker, 1970; Pattison, 1991; Sherry, 1992.

2 This and the following two paragraphs I have borrowed from Atkinson, 1996, p. 17.

3 Cf., for example, the medieval Church's manuals on *The Craft of Dying* (*Ars Moriendi*), to help the faithful cope with the fears of death, or, later and more hopeful, 'The Visitation of the Sick', in the Church of England Book of Common Prayer (1662), and also writings such as Jeremy Taylor, *Holy Dying* (1651).

4 Some of the discussion in these paragraphs is an adaptation of my chapter 'Care of the family in dying and grieving', in Spilling, 1986.

5 'Service for the Burial of the Dead', Book of Common Prayer (1662).

6 John 11.33. See my further comments in Atkinson, 1995.

Chapter 2: *Religious Experiences*

1 Some of the following paragraphs are taken from a chapter I wrote in an unpublished book presented as a gift to Dr Arthur Peacocke on his retirement as the first Warden of the Society of Ordained Scientists.

Chapter 3: *God So Loved the World*

1 Cf., for example, Jaki, 1986; 1978; Barbour, 1990; Peacocke, 1993; Hooykaas, 1972; Hodgson.

2 There is a useful and critical discussion of various forms of the anthropic principle and some of the more and some of the less sensible claims made for them in Midgley, 1994.

3 I have been much influenced by Polanyi, 1958; 1969.

4 It is of interest to compare this with Will Hutton's (1995) analysis focusing predominantly on the UK; cf. an early Christian analysis in Wolterstorff, 1983.

5 There is a growing literature on Christian attitudes to ecology. Cf. Berry, 1994; Granberg-Michaelson, 1987.

6 Cf. the very pertinent discussion of this and allied themes in Peter Selby's (1997) analysis of international and personal indebtedness which dominates personal and national life.

Chapter 4: God So Loved ... that He Gave

1 I refer to Mackie, 1977. Though I disagree with much of its assumptions, this book is a careful exercise in moral philosophy. I mention it to draw attention to the striking title, not to offer a critique of the book.

2 John 17.3 gives us a definition of eternal life: 'This is eternal life, that they know thee the only true God, and Jesus Christ whom thou hast sent.' Eternal life is the knowledge of God mediated through Jesus Christ. Eternal life is also associated with the vision of God: 'If you had known me, you would have known my Father also; henceforth you know him, and have seen him' (14.7). 'John's vision of God is neither ecstatic nor mystical; it is personal confrontation and recognition, mediated by Jesus' (Ladd, 1974, p. 263), though many writers certainly see some mystical element in the Fourth Gospel. Furthermore, eternal life is knowledge of truth. 'You will know the truth, and the truth will make you free' (8.32). Truth and life belong together for John. The Word of God is revealed 'full of grace and truth' (1.14); Jesus said 'I am the truth' (14.6). So to know the truth is to know God's purposes embodied in Christ (8.34).

3 Furthermore, all that is said of Jesus is set in an unmistakably redemptive context. He comes as 'the Saviour of the World' (4.42). The disclosing of Jesus as the Christ is also a revelation of God's judgement (9.39), but 'God sent the Son into the world, not to condemn the world, but that the world might be saved through him' (John 3.17). In other words, Christ's judgement of the world consists in this, that God's loving gift of light to the world has as its inevitable consequence the revealing of the darkness, or rather, it presents the test which reveals the fundamental bent of the heart' (Lee, 1962, p. 159). The way St John presents Jesus' crucifixion as his glorification (John 3.14; 8.28; 12.32, 34) illustrates in another way the triumph of God's love in saving the world. There is no account of Jesus' agony in the Garden of Gethsemane. The dialogue with Pilate concerns the power and authority of God (John 18.36; 19.11). His last words are

a cry of triumph, not of defeat: 'It is finished' – namely the divine work of salvation for the world. Indeed *tetelestai* has been described as 'the key word of the Fourth Gospel' (A. Corell, quoted in Morris, 1971, p. 815), by which is meant that the whole story of the Gospel is a leading up to the death of Jesus as a triumph of light over darkness, of life through death.

4 Barry goes on to say, 'but the only way in which justice can be vindicated – i.e. by arming it with force – appears to be the contradiction of love'. Cf. the discussion of love and justice in Thomas, 1955, ch. 11.

5 See my discussion in Atkinson, 1997, from which some of the following paragraphs are adapted.

6 E.g. Deuteronomy 10.17–18; 32.4, etc.; cf. fuller discussion in Atkinson, 1985, ch. 9.

Chapter 5: *His Only Son*

1 See for example, Wright, *Jesus and the Victory of God* (1996), and his more popular level *Who Was Jesus?* (1992).

2 Wright, 1985; but see the much fuller treatment in Wright, 1996.

3 I am following Wright's themes, and his headings, but adding some other material.

4 The enormously complicated questions of inter-faith dialogue, of a theology of religions, of what Christianity can learn from other world faiths, and other faiths from Christianity, of the parameters for multi-faith collaboration on issues of social justice and so on, though vitally important for the church's mission, are beyond the scope of this book. Cf. d'Costa, 1990; Cragg, 1986; Chapman, 1995; Netland, 1991.

Chapter 6: *Whoever Believes*

1 The following paragraph is loosely based on Walls, 1981, pp. 39–52, and quoted by M. Jeeves in Jeeves *et al.*, 1984.

2 Jürgen Habermas's first major book, *Knowledge and Human Interests* (1968), was the subject of significant scholarly

discussion and critique. His ideas, modified and developed, were presented in *The Theory of Communicative Action* (1984). Cf. discussion in Bernstein, 1985; Reader, 1997.
3 I am borrowing some of this discussion from Atkinson, 1990, pp. 66f.
4 To borrow the title of a book by Emil Brunner.

Chapter 7: Should Not Perish, but Have Eternal Life

1 For some of this chapter I am drawing heavily on my contribution to Goldingay, 1995.
2 In much of the following section I am drawing on Pruyser, 1991; and Oates, 1973.
3 Adapted from L. Kohlberg's developmental theory of moral capacity.
4 Haddon Wilmer sought to outline what such a political stance might involve in *Third Way* (May 1979). It was taken up by Peter Hinchlif (1982) and I have summarized it in Atkinson, 1985.
5 Church of England Book of Common Prayer, Service of Holy Communion.

Chapter 8: Towards a Missionary Theology

1 I have drawn heavily in this section on material prepared for a church working party on ministry, and have adapted it for the purposes of this book.
2 As Moltmann put it: 'The church understands its world-wide mission in the trinitarian history of God's dealings with the world. With all its activities and suffering, it is an element in the history of the kingdom of God. The real point is not to spread the church but to spread the kingdom. The goal is not the glorification of the church but the glorification of the Father through the Son in the Holy Spirit' (Moltmann, 1977, p. 11).

Or again, this time to quote Christopher Cunliffe: 'It is the task of the Church to point to God's presence in his world.

That is the only criterion, ultimately, by which the Church
has to be guided. Mission and ministry, therefore, are about
co-operating with what God is already doing in the world . . .
The Church is that community of people which confesses this
by acknowledging the lordship of Christ and is called to co-
operate with him in making all things new and pointing
others to the saving love of Christ.'

REFERENCES

Allen, D. (1989) *Christian Belief in a Postmodern World*, Louisville, KY, Westminster/John Knox Press

Allport, G (1950) *The Individual and His Religion*, London, Macmillan

Argyle, M. and Beit-Hallahmi, B. (1975) *The Social Psychology of Religion*, rev. edn, London, Routledge & Kegan Paul (first published 1958)

Atkins, P. (1994) *Creation Revisited*, Harmondsworth, Penguin

Atkinson, D. (1985) *Peace In Our Time?*, Leicester, IVP

Atkinson, D. (1990) *The Message of Genesis 1–11*, Leicester, IVP

Atkinson, D. (1993) *The Ethics of the Johannine Literature*, Southport, Christian Theology Trust

Atkinson, D. (1994) *Pastoral Ethics*, London, SPCK Lynx

Atkinson, D. (1995) 'Life, health and death', in D. Atkinson and D. Field (eds), *New Dictionary of Christian Ethics and Pastoral Theology*, Leicester, IVP

Atkinson, D. (1996) *The Message of Proverbs*, Leicester, IVP

Atkinson, D. (1997) 'A theological reflection on politics', *Anvil* 14/1

Atkinson, D. and Field, D. (eds) (1995) *New Dictionary of Christian Ethics and Pastoral Theology*, Leicester, IVP

Barbour, I. G. (1990) *Religion in an Age of Science*, London, SCM

Barry, F. R. (1966) *Christian Ethics and Secular Society*, London, Hodder & Stoughton

Barth, K. (1956–75) *Church Dogmatics*, trans. G. Bromiley *et al.*, Edinburgh, T & T Clark (first published 1932)

Batson, C. D. and Ventis, W. L. (1982) *The Religious Experience*, Oxford, Oxford University Press

Becker, E. (1973) *The Denial of Death*, London and New York, Macmillan

Berger, P. (1969) *A Rumour of Angels*, New York, Doubleday

Bernstein, R. (1983) *Beyond Objectivism and Relativism*, Philadelphia, University of Philadelphia Press

Bernstein, R. (1991) *The New Constellations: The Ethical-Political Horizons of Modernity/Postmodernity*, Cambridge, Polity Press

Bernstein, R. (ed.) (1985) *Habermas and Modernity*, Cambridge and Oxford, Polity Press and Blackwell

Berry, R. J. (1994) 'Green religion and green science', in D. Atkinson (ed.), *Pastoral Ethics*, London, SPCK Lynx

Bomford, R. (1996) 'Models of ministry: from management and magic to the making of the Kingdom', *Affirming Catholicism* 22, 22

Bonhoeffer, D. (1959) *Creation and Fall* (ET), London, SCM (first published 1937)

Bosch, D. (1992) *Transforming Mission*, Maryknoll, NY, Orbis Books

Bowker, J. (1973) *The Sense of God*, Oxford, Clarendon

Buber, M. (1970) *I and Thou*, Edinburgh, T & T Clark

Calvin, J. (1536) *Institutes of the Christian Religion*

Chapman, C. (1995) *Cross and Crescent*, Leicester, IVP

Cragg, K. (1986) *The Christ and the Faiths*, Philadelphia, Westminster Press

Cunliffe, C. unpublished paper

Davie, G. (1994) *Religion in Britain since 1945: Believing without Belonging*, Oxford, Blackwell

Dawkins, R. (1978) *The Selfish Gene*, London, Granada

Dawkins, R. (1991) *The Blind Watchmaker*, Harmondsworth, Penguin

d'Costa, G. (ed.) (1990) *Christian Uniqueness Reconsidered*, Maryknoll, NY, Orbis Books

Derrida, J. (1978) *Writing and Difference*, trans. Alan Bass, London, Routledge & Kegan Paul (first published 1967)

Dowell, G. (1990) *Enjoying the World: The Rediscovery of Thomas Traherne*, London, Mowbray

Dykstra, C. (1981) *Vision and Character*, New York, Paulist Press

Edwards, Jonathan (1746) *A Treatise Concerning Religious Affections*

Eliot, T. S. (1974) *The Four Quartets*, 'Burnt Norton', in *Collected Poems, 1909–1962*, London, Faber & Faber

Erikson, E. (1951) 'The eight ages of man', in *Childhood and Society*, London, Imago

Faber, H. (1976) *Psychology of Religion*, London, SCM

Forsyth, P. T. (1911) *Christ on Parnassus*, London, Hodder & Stoughton

Gardner, W. H. (1970) 'Introduction', in Gerard Manley Hopkins, *Poems and Prose*, ed. W. H. Gardner, London, Penguin

Geffroy, G. (1922) *Monet: sa vie, son temps, son oeuvre*, Paris

Gennep, Arnold van (1960) *Rites of Passage*, Chicago, University of Chicago Press

Glasser, W. (1965) *Reality Therapy*, New York, Harper & Row

Gleick, J. (1987) *Chaos*, London, Cardinal Books

Goldingay, J. (ed.) (1995) *Atonement Today*, London, SPCK

Gombrich, E. H. (1979) *Ideals and Idols*, London, Phaidon

Gombrich, E. H. (1995) *The Story of Art*, London, Phaidon (first published 1950)

Granberg-Michaelson, W. (ed.) (1987) *Tending the Garden*, Grand Rapids, Eerdmans

Gregoire, S. (1994) *Monet*, Paris, Hazan

Gunton, C. (1985) *Enlightenment and Alienation*, London, Marshall, Morgan & Scott

Habermas, J. (1984) *The Theory of Communicative Action* (ET), vol. I, Boston

Habermas, J. (1987) *Knowledge and Human Interests*, trans. J. J. Shapiro, Cambridge and Oxford, Polity Press and Blackwell

Hardy, A. (1979) *The Spiritual Nature of Man*, Oxford, Clarendon

Harries, R. (1993) *Art and the Beauty of God*, London, Mowbray

Hart, K. (1989) *The Trespass of the Sign*, Cambridge, Cambridge University Press

Harvey, D. (1989) *The Condition of Postmodernity*, 2nd edn, Oxford, Blackwell

Hay, D. (1982) *Exploring Inner Space*, Harmondsworth, Penguin

Hay, D. (1990) *Religious Experience Today*, London, Mowbray

Herbert, G. (1981) *George Herbert: The Country Parson, The Temple*, ed. J. N. Wall Jr, Classics of Western Spirituality, New York, Paulist Press (poems first published 1633)

Hinchlif, P. (1982) *Holiness and Politics*, London, Darton, Longman & Todd

Hobbes, T. (1651) *Leviathan*

Hodgson, P. various papers for the Farmington Institute, Oxford

Hood, R. W. (1991) 'Mysticism in the psychology of religion', in N. Malony (ed.), *Psychology of Religion: Personalities, Problems, Possibilities*, Grand Rapids, Baker Book House

Hooykaas, R. (1972) *Religion and the Rise of Modern Science*, Edinburgh, Scottish Academic Press

Hutton, W. (1995) *The State We're In*, London, Jonathan Cape

Irenaeus (1868) (second century) *The Writings of Irenaeus*, vol. I: *Against Heresies*, trans. A. Roberts and W. H. Rambaut, The Ante-Nicene Fathers, Edinburgh, T & T Clark

Jaki, S. (1978) *The Road of Science and the Ways to God*, Edinburgh, Scottish Academic Press

Jaki, S. (1983) *Angels, Apes and Men*, La Salle, IL, Sherwood Sugden & Co

Jaki, S. (1986) *Science and Creation*, Edinburgh, Scottish Academic Press

James, W. (1952) *The Varieties of Religious Experience*, London, Longman Green & Co. (first published 1902)

Jeeves, M., Berry, R. J. and Atkinson, D. (eds) (1984) *Free To Be Different*, London, Marshall, Morgan & Scott

John Paul II (1994) *Tertio Millennio Adveniente*, London, Catholic Truth Society

Kierkegaard, S. (1847) *Works of Love*

Klein, M. (1975) 'Our adult world and its roots in infancy', in *Envy and Gratitude*, London, Hogarth Press (first published 1959)

Küng, Hans (1977) *On Being a Christian*, trans. E. Quinn, London, Collins

Küng, Hans (1992) *Mozart*, London, SCM

Ladd, G. E. (1974) *A Theology of the New Testament*, Guildford and London, Lutterworth

Lakeland, P. (1997) *Postmodernity: Christian Identity in a Fragmented Age*, Minneapolis, Fortress

Lambeth Conference (1988) *The Truth Shall Make You Free*

Lash, N. (1986) *Easter in Ordinary*, Notre Dame and London, University of Notre Dame Press

Leaver, R. (1981) *Music as Preaching: Bach, Passions and Music in Worship*, Oxford, Latimer House

Lee, E. K. (1962) *The Religious Thought of St John*, London, SPCK

Leech, K. (1997) *The Sky is Red*, London, Darton, Longman & Todd

Lewis, C. S. (1943) *The Abolition of Man*, Oxford, Oxford University Press

Lewis, H. D. (1970) *Our Experience of God*, London, Collins Fontana (first published 1959)

Locke, J. (1690) *Two Treatises on Civil Government*

Logan, P. (1997) *Biblical Reflections on the Political Economy of Jubilee*, Southwark Diocesan Board for Church in Society

Lovell, B. (1977) F. W. Angel Memorial Lecture

Lyon, J. (1994) *Postmodernity*, Buckingham, Open University Press

Lyotard, J.-F. (1992) *The Post-Modern Condition: A Report on Knowledge*, Manchester, Manchester University Press

McGrath, A. (1992) *Bridge-Building*, Leicester, IVP

MacIntyre, A. (1981) *After Virtue*, London, Duckworth

McKeating, H. (1970) *Living with Guilt*, London, SCM

Mackie, J. L. (1977) *Ethics: Inventing Right and Wrong*, Harmondsworth, Penguin

Macmurray, J. (1961) *Persons in Relation*, London, Faber & Faber

Mayne, M. (1995) *This Sunrise of Wonder*, London, Fount

Midgley, M. (1994) *Science as Salvation*, London, Routledge

Moltmann, J. (1977) *The Church in the Power of the Spirit*, trans. M. Kohl, London, SCM

Morea, P. (1990) *Personality*, Harmondsworth, Penguin

Morris, L. (1971) *The Gospel According to John*, London, Marshall, Morgan & Scott

Morris, L. (1989) *The Cross of Jesus*, Exeter, Paternoster

Murdoch, I. (1990) *The Message to the Planet*, Harmondsworth, Penguin

Neill, S. (1959) *A Genuinely Human Existence*, London, Constable

Netland, H. (1991) *Dissonant Voices: Religious Pluralism and the Question of Truth*, Grand Rapids, Eerdmans

Niebuhr, H. R. (1963) *The Responsible Self*, New York, Harper & Row

Niebuhr, R. (1945) *Children of Light and Children of Darkness*, London, Nisbet

Oates, W. (1973) *The Psychology of Religion*, Waco, Word Books

Owen, H. P. (1965) *The Moral Argument for Christian Theism*, London, Allen & Unwin

Paine, T. (1791) *The Rights of Man*

Pascal, B. (1670) *Pensées*

Pattison, G. (1991) *Art, Modernity and Faith*, London, SCM

Peacocke, A. R. (1971) *Science and the Christian Experiment*, Oxford, Oxford University Press

Peacocke, A. R. (1979) *Creation and the World of Science*, Oxford, Clarendon

Peacocke, A. R. (1984) *Intimations of Reality*, Notre Dame, University of Notre Dame Press

Peacocke, A. R. (1993) *Theology for a Scientific Age*, London, SCM

Philipps, A. C. J. (1970) *Ancient Israel's Criminal Law*, Oxford, Blackwell

Pincus, L. (1976) *Death and the Family*, London, Faber

Polanyi, M. (1958) *Personal Knowledge*, London, Routledge & Kegan Paul

Polanyi, M. (1966) *The Tacit Dimension*, New York, Doubleday

Polanyi, M. (1969) *Knowing and Being*, London, Routledge & Kegan Paul

Polanyi, M. and Prosch, H. (1975) *Meaning*, Chicago and London, University of Chicago Press

Polkinghorne, J. (1986) *One World*, London, SPCK

Polkinghorne, J. (1988) *Science and Creation*, London, SPCK

Polkinghorne, J. (1989) *Science and Providence*, London, SPCK

Polkinghorne, J. (1991) *Reason and Reality*, London, SPCK

Polkinghorne, J. (1994) *Science and Christian Belief* (The Gifford Lectures for 1993–4), London, SPCK

Pruyser, P. W. (1991) 'Anxiety, guilt and shame in the atonement', in H. Newton Malony and B. Spilka (eds), *Religion in Psychodynamic Perspective*, Oxford, Oxford University Press

Rabinow, P. (ed.) (1984) *The Foucault Reader*, Harmondsworth, Penguin

Ramsey, P. (1950) *Basic Christian Ethics*, London, SCM

Reader, J. (1997) *Beyond All Reason: The Limits of Postmodern Theology*, Cardiff, Aureus

Real World Coalition (1996) *The Politics of the Real World*, London, Earthscan

Rookmaaker, H. (1970) *Modern Art and the Death of a Culture*, Leicester, IVP

Rorty, R. (1991) *Objectivity, Relativism and Truth*, Cambridge, Cambridge University Press

Rousseau, J.-J. (1762) *Du Contrat Social*

Rowley, H. H. (1956) *The Faith of Israel*, London, SCM

Sacks, J. (1995) *Faith in the Future*, London, Darton, Longman & Todd

Selby, P. (1997) *Grace and Mortgage*, London, Darton, Longman & Todd

Sherry, P. (1992) *Spirit and Beauty: An Introduction to Theological Aesthetics*, Oxford, Clarendon

Spilling, R. (ed.) (1986) *Terminal Care at Home*, Oxford, Oxford University Press

Strunk, O. (1980) 'Contributions to research method', in J. R. Tisdale (ed.), *Growing Edges in the Psychology of Religion*, Chicago, Nelson Hall

Suttie, I. (1988) *The Origins of Love and Hate*, London, Free Association Books (first published 1935)

Taylor, C. (1989) *Sources of the Self*, Cambridge, Cambridge University Press

Taylor, C. (1991) *The Ethics of Authenticity*, Cambridge, MA, Harvard University Press

Temple, W. (1934) *Nature, Man and God*, London, Macmillan

Thielicke, H. (1969) *I Believe*, London, Collins

Thielicke, H. (1983) *Living with Death*, Grand Rapids, Eerdmans

Thiselton, A. (1995) *Interpreting God and the Post-Modern Self*, Edinburgh, T & T Clark

Thomas, G. F. (1955) *Christian Ethics and Moral Philosophy*, New York, Scribners

Thorson, W. R. (1978) 'The spiritual dimensions of science', in C. F. H. Henry (ed.), *Horizons of Science*, New York, Harper & Row

Torrance, T. F. (1971) *God and Rationality*, Oxford, Oxford University Press

Torrance, T. F. (1980) *The Ground and Grammar of Theology*, Belfast, Christian Journals

Traherne, T. (1675) *Christian Ethicks*

Traherne, T. (1908) *Centuries of Meditations*, ed. B. Dobell, London, B. Dobell

Waldrop, M. M. (1992) *Complexity* (written in the late 17th century), Harmondsworth, Penguin

Walls, A. (1981) 'The gospel as the prisoner and liberator of culture', *Faith and Thought* 108/1 & 2, 39–52

Walker, A. (1996) *Telling the Story: Gospel Mission and Culture*, London, SPCK

Ward, K. (1996) *God, Chance and Necessity*, Oxford, Oneworld

Watts, F. and Williams, M. (1988) *The Psychology of Religious Knowing*, Cambridge, Cambridge University Press

Weber, M. (1992) *The Protestant Ethic and the Spirit of Capitalism*, London, Routledge (first published 1920)

Webster, J. (1995) 'God', in D. Atkinson and D. Field (eds), *New Dictionary of Christian Ethics and Pastoral Theology*, Leicester, IVP

Weil, Simone (1952) *Gravity and Grace* (ET), London, Routledge (first published 1947)

Weil, Simone (1977) *Waiting on God*, trans. E. Crauford, London, Fount (first published 1950)

Williams, S. (1981) *Politics Is For People*, London, Allen Lane

Winnicott, D. W. (1974) 'Transitional objects and transitional phenomena', in *Playing and Reality*, Harmondsworth, Penguin

Wolterstorff, N. (1980) *Art in Action: Towards a Christian Aesthetic*, Grand Rapids, Eerdmans

Wolterstorff, N. (1983) *Until Justice and Peace Embrace*, Grand Rapids, Eerdmans

Wright, C. J. H. (1990) *God's People in God's Land*, Grand Rapids, Eerdmans

Wright, N. T. (1985) 'Jesus, Israel and the cross', Society of Biblical Literature Seminar Papers

Wright, N. T. (1992) *Who Was Jesus?*, London, SPCK

Wright, N. T. (1996) *Jesus and the Victory of God*, London, SPCK

Young, F. (1982) *Can These Dry Bones Live?*, London, SCM

Zizioulas, J. (1985) *Being as Communion*, London, Darton, Longman & Todd

The Society for Promoting Christian Knowledge (SPCK) has as its purpose three main tasks:

- **Communicating the Christian faith in its rich diversity**
- **Helping people to understand the Christian faith and to develop their personal faith**
- **Equipping Christians for mission and ministry**

SPCK Worldwide serves the Church through Christian literature and communication projects in over 100 countries. Special schemes also provide books for those training for ministry in many parts of the developing world. SPCK Worldwide's ministry involves Churches of many traditions. This worldwide service depends upon the generosity of others and all gifts are spent wholly on ministry programmes, without deductions.

SPCK Bookshops support the life of the Christian community by making available a full range of Christian literature and other resources, and by providing support to bookstalls and book agents throughout the UK. SPCK Bookshops' mail order department meets the needs of overseas customers and those unable to have access to local bookshops.

SPCK Publishing produces Christian books and resources, covering a wide range of inspirational, pastoral, practical and academic subjects. Authors are drawn from many different Christian traditions, and publications aim to meet the needs of a wide variety of readers in the UK and throughout the world.

The Society does not necessarily endorse the individual views contained in its publications, but hopes they stimulate readers to think about and further develop their Christian faith.

For further information about the Society, please write to:

SPCK, Holy Trinity Church, Marylebone Road,
London NW1 4DU, United Kingdom.
Telephone: 0171 387 5282